History Strikes Back

History Strikes Back

How States, Nations, and Conflicts Are Shaping the Twenty-First Century

Hubert Védrine

Translated by Philip H. Gordon

BROOKINGS INSTITUTION PRESS
Washington, D.C.

Originally published as *Continuer l'Histoire*
Copyright © 2007 Libraire Arthème Fayard

Copyright © 2008
THE BROOKINGS INSTITUTION
1775 Massachusetts Avenue, N.W., Washington, D.C. 20036
www.brookings.edu

Library of Congress Cataloging-in-Publication data

Védrine, Hubert.
   [Continuer l'histoire. English]
   History strikes back : how states, nations, and conflicts are shaping the twenty-first century / Hubert Védrine ; translated by Philip H. Gordon ; foreword by Madeleine Albright.
       p. cm.
   Translated from the French.
   Includes index.
   Summary: "Offers an overview of world politics since the fall of the Berlin Wall. Takes issue with the belief that states are unnecessary and globalization and free markets will make a better world. Promotes a 'smart Realpolitik' to guide West relations with emerging powers, manage globalization, and deal with environmental challenges"—Provided by publisher.
   ISBN 978-0-8157-8984-0 (cloth : alk. paper)
   1. Balance of power. 2. International relations. 3. World politics—21st century. I. Title.
JZ1313.V4318 2008
909.83—dc22   2008037978

9 8 7 6 5 4 3 2 1

Printed on acid-free paper

Typeset in Adobe Garamond

Composition by Cynthia Stock
Silver Spring, Maryland

Printed by R. R. Donnelley
Harrisonburg, Virginia

Contents

Foreword

In 1999 NATO blocked Yugoslav dictator Slobodan Miloševiç's brutal attempt to expel much of Kosovo's ethnic Albanian population from its homeland. The decision to intervene was made without explicit authorization from the UN Security Council and was condemned by critics as a violation of Yugoslav sovereignty. Because NATO acts by consensus, this humanitarian action could not have taken place without the support of French Foreign Minister Hubert Védrine, and yet endorsing it ran contrary to some of Védrine's strongest instincts. As a supporter of international law, Védrine was hesitant to undermine the prestige of the Security Council, which in this case could not act because of a threatened Russian veto. As a realist, the foreign minister was wary of moral outrage as a trigger for military action because he believed that self-righteousness and wisdom are often at odds—and that moral intentions are no guarantee of moral results. Finally, as a defender of Gallic pride, Védrine inevitably had qualms about an operation viewed by many around the world as a confirmation of America's post–cold war leadership.

So why did Védrine support intervention in Kosovo? The answer, quite simply, is that it was the right thing to do. Neither the United States, nor France, nor our other allies were prepared to stand by and watch as thousands of innocent people were killed or made homeless in the heart of Europe. NATO's action served the cause of justice, saved many lives, and presaged an end to Miloševiç's disastrous political reign. These beneficial outcomes do not mean that Védrine's initial reservations about the operation lacked merit. Through the rigor of his questions, Védrine made clear that Kosovo should be considered an exceptional case, not a precedent for future actions. America had been given no general license to take NATO support for granted, rely too much on military solutions, or disregard the prerogatives of the UN. To avert bloodshed in Kosovo, Védrine was flexible in applying his principles, but he did not abandon those principles. A few years later, in Iraq, the types of concerns he had raised about the Kosovo intervention were wholly disregarded, at great cost to us all.

During my years as America's secretary of state (1997–2001), I never ignored Védrine's perspective. Even if I had tried, he would not have let me. Hubert insisted on having his say, and whenever he spoke, he did so exceptionally well. Conversing with Védrine was like kayaking down a fast-flowing river. There was enough movement to demand concentration, enough excitement to keep spirits high, and enough danger to prevent complacency. As a result, he was my favorite diplomat with whom to disagree.

Whether we were conferring in Paris or Washington, we rarely viewed an issue in precisely the same terms, but neither did we argue so strongly that communication became impossible. Védrine is an intellectual who is ever-conscious of the broad currents of history; I am more of a problem-solver who operates primarily in the here and now. I admired Hubert because he didn't mince his words; he appreciated me because I replied to his words in French.

Usually our exchanges focused on the crisis of the moment. On less urgent occasions we were able to deal more generally with the affectionate yet touchy relationship between our two countries. While I emphasized our nations' shared interests, Hubert made plain his distress that the trend toward globalization was being driven by Anglo-Saxons. While I emphasized America's agenda within the context of the Euro-Atlantic partnership, he was a fierce defender of France's leadership role within Europe. When I pointed to Lafayette as an inspiration for Franco-American solidarity, Védrine smiled and replied, "Ah, but you see, *chère* Madeleine, Lafayette did not cross the Atlantic to help the Americans; his motive was to defeat the British."

Now that we are both out of office, we still meet and speak but have found less to argue about and more about which to worry. In this decade, al Qaeda has emerged as a significant threat; the wars in Iraq and Afghanistan have strained NATO unity; progress toward Arab-Israeli peace has stalled; environmental and energy challenges have been neglected; and the global divide between rich and poor has widened. Meanwhile, the international nuclear non-proliferation regime has weakened, multilateral institutions are showing their age, and rising food and fuel prices are battering the world economy. All this provides abundant material for thoughtful analysis and debate.

There is, of course, no shortage of experts offering their opinions about world affairs. The difference between a former foreign minister such as Hubert Védrine and a commentator from the realms of academia or journalism is that Védrine has experienced the pressures of practical decisionmaking. His views have been tested in the unforgiving environment of domestic and international politics, where every statement is dissected and every miscalculation exposed. As a writer, Védrine blends the insights of a skilled practitioner with the thematic scope of a creative theorist. The provocative results are evident in each fascinating chapter of *History Strikes Back,* a volume written just as Western leadership was shifting from one quartet (Blair, Chirac, Schroeder, and Bush) to the next (Brown, Sarkozy, Merkel, and either Obama or McCain).

In these pages, Védrine does not attempt to lay out a detailed blueprint for the future. He does, however, recommend a few changes in attitude.

To begin, America must recognize that it is respected less now than it was only a decade ago. In Védrine's view, America's new president would be well advised to help strengthen multilateral institutions rather than try to work around them as his predecessor did so unsuccessfully.

Europeans, meanwhile, must understand that solutions to global problems cannot be found by relying on a benign and cohesive "international community" that does not actually exist. Védrine argues that the popular belief that nation-states have become irrelevant is belied by inescapable facts. The major plagues of our era—such as terror, strife, poverty, climate change, and disease—can be addressed effectively only if national governments are both capable and engaged.

According to Védrine, leaders on both sides of the Atlantic must accept the fact that the axis of global power is shifting. The three-fourths of the world's inhabitants who are neither European nor American are busy organizing themselves. They are not waiting for a divided West to lead. It follows that the institutions established by the West after World War II are due for a makeover.

Finally, Védrine counsels us all to steer clear of enthusiasms that promise more than they can deliver. He refers, in particular, to America's penchant for "democratic Messianism" and Europe's tendency to embrace "multilateral fundamentalism." To Védrine, it is folly to believe that faith in a particular doctrine—however uplifting—will obviate the need for intelligent and nuanced action.

In every chapter of this volume, Hubert Védrine challenges our illusions. He demands that we see the world as it is, not because he wants us to accept the status quo, but because we will never engineer the right kind of change if our actions are based on false premises. Those who think too highly of their own moral purity, or who place too much faith in the altruism of others, are doomed to disappointment. The same is true of those who believe that goodwill alone can provide a stable foundation for global politics.

Védrine urges us to develop an international system that accommodates national interests within a framework that encourages decency and civility but anticipates neither saintliness nor consistency. An imperfect world demands arrangements that can absorb flaws without surrendering to them. Only if we reserve our indignation for the issues that matter most will we be able to forge international policies that deal effectively with the gravest problems.

Although Védrine is skeptical of American leadership, he fully accepts the world's ongoing need for an articulate guiding voice. He does not expect the election of a new U.S. president to heal all ills, but he does hold out hope that a change in the White House will restore a broader sense of common purpose within the West. Such a restoration is most likely if the new president is knowledgeable about history and culture, aware of the limits of U.S. power, and conscious of the complexity of global relationships.

I heartily recommend *History Strikes Back* not because I agree with every sentence, but because every sentence is worth reading whether as a source of information, an invitation to debate, or a rebuttal to easy assumptions. This is a work of remarkable intelligence at a moment when critical thinking is essential and history is moving ahead at full throttle. My invitation to you is to read and ponder this timely volume; you will enjoy doing so and will end up considerably wiser than when you began.

Madeleine K. Albright

August 2008

History Strikes Back

CHAPTER ONE

The West in Disarray

When the cold war came to an end, many in the West assumed they were the winners, the new Masters of the Universe. That's why they are now so disoriented by a world that is turning out to be very different from the one they expected.

In the early 1990s, after undeniable success in a forty-five-year-long struggle against the Soviet Union, Westerners became intoxicated with their victory. In the United States, the mood was one of unabated triumphalism. President George H. W. Bush talked about creating a "new world order" that would last for decades and serve the interests of all mankind. Francis Fukuyama, then still a neoconservative, announced the "end of History" on the grounds that the victorious West could no longer be challenged by any rival ideology or power. Western values—such as the market economy and democracy—would be extended irresistibly throughout the world. After all, hadn't even China's Communist leader Deng Xiaoping, in the late 1970s, embraced the market economy? The common assumption was that nothing could stop the advance of democracy and liberalism.

The 1993 warnings of Samuel Huntington, who, on the contrary, thought that the new world would be threatened by a "clash of civilizations," were all but forgotten. Huntington's message was dismissed as too disturbing, too politically incorrect, too distant from the prevailing American self-assurance and European optimism. Huntington identified nine civilizations: Western, Latin American, African, Islamic, Chinese, Hindu, Orthodox, Buddhist, and Japanese. Critics nitpicked his categories and challenged the notion that civilizations were "clashing." Weren't we all brothers and sisters?

Nevertheless, Americans believed their leadership and benevolent hegemony to be more necessary than ever for global stability and security. The more innocent Europeans and Canadians, on the other hand, were keen to start cashing in their peace dividends. They believed that the end of the cold war would lead to the birth of a true "international community." Despite the failures of the post–World War I "league" of nations and the post–World War II "united" nations, this time a true community of nations would be born. Within it, all states would share the same, Western-inspired values, now recognized as universal. They would work together according to the rules of multilateralism, which would give smaller states a voice and allow the majority to make decisions in the general interest. The few holdouts—so-called rogue states—would be marginalized and, if necessary, dealt with more forcefully. Conflicts would be foreseen and major problems addressed by the United Nations Security Council, which would finally be able to play its proper role, just as it did when its five permanent members legally and legitimately authorized the 1991 war to liberate Kuwait. The rare wars that did take place would be wars of "zero deaths," at least on the Western side. International law would develop, denying impunity to war criminals and deterring new crimes. "International civil society" would become increasingly influential, forcing states to be more transparent, ethical, and moral. In some areas, international civil society and nongovernmental organizations (NGOs) would even take over the role of states.

Among Europeans, as well as among some American Democrats, the idea took hold that traditional state-to-state international relations were outmoded. *Realpolitik*—according to the dictionary a policy based on the balance of power with no regard for ideology—was rejected indignantly as having been responsible for the horrors of the twentieth century. The idea was to replace it with multilateral "global governance" by "new actors" (such as civil society, NGOs, the media, and international lawyers), free trade, and human rights diplomacy. During the 1990s, gigantic UN summits—political versions of high mass—brought together the nearly 200 UN member states to deal with the environment (Rio de Janeiro, in 1992), social development (Copenhagen, 1995), the role of women in society (Beijing, 1995), and other issues. Everyone thought that this sort of multilateralism was the right method for dealing with "global challenges."

This optimism culminated in the so called "Millennium Declaration," adopted on September 8, 2000, by all the member states of the UN. In this thirty-two-point statement, we were reminded that "the United Nations is the indispensable common house of the entire human family, through which we will seek to realize our universal aspirations for peace, cooperation and development." The text outlines the fundamental values on which international relations in the twenty-first century must be based—liberty, equality, solidarity, tolerance, respect for nature, and shared responsibility. Who could possibly be against any of that?

As for globalization, the elites saw only its positive side, which would allow world trade to open up each part of the world to the others. Ending protectionism would tear down the barriers between peoples, reduce tensions over identity, and eliminate the tendency to look inward. Globalization would generate unprecedented global economic growth. Everyone, all individuals and all nations, would benefit—a "win-win" situation, as Americans like to say—giving birth to an integrated global culture somewhat like the "fusion" cuisine you can get in good restaurants in New York or Shanghai.

One major consequence of the West's feeling of superiority—and Manichaean worldview—was that foreign policy became superfluous. After all, since the West had won, why bother to negotiate with repugnant regimes? Why deal with despots? Why seek to compromise with dictators when Western values would be imposed on them whether they liked it or not, by choice or by force? All we had to do was threaten, lecture, and penalize the holdouts. Public opinion, the media, and Western NGOs would rise up in indignation every time the need to resolve some conflict led diplomats or political leaders to deal with an undemocratic regime in Asia, Africa, or the Arab world (or even with Putin's Russia). In the name of some higher morality—a form of diplomatic puritanism—they would criticize states that were allegedly blinded by *realpolitik* or commercial interests. "How dare you speak to that dictator!?" "How can you possibly trust such a government!?" And, as if there were really a choice between the two, "How can you choose business deals over human rights!?"

These illusions took various forms in the United States, and they were different from—even contradictory to—their forms in Europe. The divergence of the United States and Europe can be traced to the evolution of a set of ideas that first appeared in the United States.

From 1989 to 1992, George H. W. Bush and his foreign policy team—in particular, Secretary of State James Baker and National Security Adviser Brent Scowcroft—pursued a classic form of American leadership. Following in a long Republican tradition, its hallmarks were realism and strength without too much arrogance, sermonizing, or belligerence. America came across as a sort of "reluctant sheriff," to borrow a term from former Bush foreign policy official Richard Haass. Together with Helmut Kohl,

François Mitterrand, and Mikhail Gorbachev, the Bush team oversaw the collapse of the Soviet Union and the end of the bipolar era of global power with determination and a sense of responsibility. In the 1990 Gulf War, they stuck closely to the mandate authorized by the United Nations—to liberate Kuwait, and when that job was done they focused immediately on the Arab-Israeli peace process.

During President Bill Clinton's two terms in office (1993–2000), American power expanded, economically as well as politically. Indeed, it came to dominate world affairs so thoroughly that the old term "superpower" no longer seemed to suffice. That's why, in 1998, well before Bush's election, I coined the term "hyperpower" to evoke the United States' unprecedented power and influence. In French, the prefix "hyper" is descriptive, not judgmental. I did not coin the term to criticize or condemn the United States, but simply to describe a reality and to issue a warning about the consequences of such dominance.

Clinton managed to make the immense power of the United States seem acceptable to the rest of the world. He did it through his exceptional sense of global political realities—a rare quality among American political leaders—as well as through his charisma and openness and his belated but sincere efforts to bring about Middle East peace. As president, he managed to contain a desire for hegemony that was deeply ingrained in the attitudes of the American public, the U.S. media, and certain think tanks.

The Republican Party had by 1994 become highly reactionary, and its victories in the congressional elections that year demonstrated how strong the hegemonic impulse had become. The party's new mantra was marked by rigid nationalism; the reassertion of national interests; opposition to any limits on national sovereignty; a ruthless conception of relations with allies that was hierarchical, unilateralist, and exploitative; and the belief in a purely military approach to conflict resolution. The Republican victory in 1994 signaled a harder line than the one embodied in Ronald Reagan's slogan "America is back." George W. Bush's own slogan, unveiled on September 12, 2001—"We have found our mission"—would confirm that harder line.

The transformation of the Republican Party had deep roots. In the 1960s, southern, working-class whites, appalled by President Johnson's policy of racial desegregation, abandoned Roosevelt's Democratic Party and joined the Republicans, tipping it toward right-wing populism thirty years later. That populism was further hardened by a powerful evangelical movement estimated to represent some 40 million people. The movement's literalist reading of the Bible leads it to align itself with an Israeli Far Right that opposes any sort of territorial compromise, a great irony given the ideological and racist traditions in much of the southern United States itself. At the same time, some Republican elites began to join the neoconservative movement. The movement was misnamed, because the former leftists who joined it—many initially had been Democrats, intellectuals, and Trotskyites—did not become conservatives but, instead, reactionary revolutionaries. During the cold war, they had fought tooth and nail against the détente policies of their bête noire, Henry Kissinger, whom they saw as too soft on the Soviet Union and other enemies of the United States. They viewed Ronald Reagan as a gift from above, grudgingly endured the realism of the first President Bush, and attacked President Clinton personally and politically in every conceivable way. They criticized Clinton for failing to win the world's respect for America, for refusing to use force to overthrow Saddam Hussein, for weakening America's global authority in a futile search for Middle East peace, and, finally, for tarnishing the presidency with the Lewinsky affair.

These "neocons," initially led, in the 1970s, by Senator Henry "Scoop" Jackson and his aide Richard Perle, argued that there was no such thing as a Palestinian problem, which they saw as an invention of an irrelevant Israeli Left and of anti-Israeli groups the world over. Remarkably, they pedaled this view even when the Oslo peace process was in full swing. Their alternative solution was to democratize—whether the locals liked it or not—the neighboring Arab countries, which, they somehow believed, would make those countries pro-Western and pro-Israeli. That process would allow the Israelis to keep the occupied territories, as desired by Likud, the right-wing party created by Menachem Begin in 1973. Perle and others spelled out this attempt to get around the Palestinian problem in a 1996 publication called *A Clean Break: A New Strategy for Securing the Realm.* Their approach continues to this day to have serious consequences for the situation in the Middle East, Israel's security, and relations between the West and the Arab and Muslim worlds while leading U.S. foreign policy to a dead end.

The neocons creatively grafted Woodrow Wilson's democratic messianism—which had so irritated Clemenceau in Paris in 1919 and still today dominates Western thinking—onto the nationalist American tradition of Theodore Roosevelt and William Taft. Before the election of George W. Bush and the Iraqi quagmire that followed it, this unique worldview enjoyed wide influence in the United States, affecting even some Democrats and the public at large. Vietnam had been forgotten. With the fall of the Soviet Union, Americans had once again found confidence in their Manifest Destiny.

To the American public (and to Europeans as well, for that matter), democratizing the world seemed to be an urgent and realistic task, not to be questioned, Madeleine Albright, Clinton's remarkable and dynamic secretary of state, organized a conference in Warsaw in June 2000 for representatives of about 100 countries to found a "Community of Democracies." And even now, despite the Iraq fiasco, Senator John McCain talks about creating a "League of Democracies." After all, if democracy is the near-term end state for all the world's peoples, and if Westerners are destined to be its vanguard, why wait? Why not just overthrow the rogue regimes? And why allow despots at the UN to insult you or prevent you from taking action?

Albright wasn't alone in her belief that democracy could be spread rapidly and successfully around the world. American strategists had already been tempted to try to pursue the democratization project through an enlarged NATO—which had become a sort of mini-UN they could control. The NATO strategy was just the most recent expression of the vision expressed by Winston Churchill to Eisenhower's first secretary of state, John Foster Dulles: "Only the English-speaking peoples count; together they can run the world."

In 2003 Europeans believed themselves to be entirely opposed to Bush and to what French scholar Pierre Hassner has called "Wilsonianism in army boots." In reality, they largely shared a belief in the West's democratization mission. The French public was highly sympathetic to the notion of the West's "right"—or even its "duty"—to intervene, as embodied by Bernard Kouchner, the founder of Doctors without Borders, who became French foreign minister in 2007. The rise of this notion was nothing less than the rehabilitation of the *mission civilisatrice* that European colonialists used to invoke but which had been forgotten since decolonization. Much of the news media took it upon themselves to ensure that this democratizing activism remained the top priority for Western foreign policy.

Where Americans and Europeans disagreed was over the question of the use of force. Since 1945, and even more so since 1989, Europeans have believed that they live in a post-tragic, posthistorical, and for federalists, even postnational world. Theirs is an ideal world, democratic and peaceful, governed by universal values, norms, and laws and by collective means of security and conflict prevention. In a sense, they dream of a world populated only by western Europeans. They have adopted a simplified form of the notion of "soft power" formulated by American professor Joseph Nye, the difference being that Nye never believed that soft power alone would suffice. At the same time, and in an entirely contradictory way, they believe it imperative (proselytizing in a manner as old as Christianity itself) that they impose their values on everyone else. For Europeans today, speeches, conditionality, sanctions, and interference are all acceptable and legitimate, whereas war, bombing, and military occupation are not, even if legally authorized. Americans, in contrast, accept the use of force and consider it legitimate (because it's *their* force) even as they debate the means used. They often even find it admirable to "go it alone," in contrast to Europeans (with the exception of some European neocon imitators), for whom the use of force must be based on a legitimate, multilateral decision—an attitude Americans of the Bush years denounced as a form of appeasement. This division is the source of the split between the Americans and Europeans over the Iraq war. The American neoconservative writer Robert Kagan was not wrong, in 2002, to characterize this difference as one between Mars (the United States) and Venus (Europe).

Except for these differences over the use of force, which were exacerbated by the Iraq adventure, Westerners today largely share the same beliefs in the universal values of democracy—or rather the same illusions about their ability to bring it about from the outside. My point is not that the basic rights called for in the United States, Britain, and France at the end of the eighteenth century—and taken up in the Universal Declaration of Human

Rights in 1948—do not express a deep and universal human aspiration. No one, in any culture, wants to be deprived of liberty, let alone abused or murdered. Moreover, many non-Western figures, such as Nobel Prize winners Amartya Sen, Mohammed Yunus, and Shirin Ebadi, defend such rights. But when we fight against the relativism of concepts like "Muslim values" or "Asian values," we fail to see that some of our principles are construed by many not as universal rights but as tools for extending Western supremacy. Many of those living in the developing world—what used to be called the "South"—have longer memories than we do, and they do not find all our recent and very convenient self-forgiveness (particularly among Europeans) very convincing. They remember that the West often violated its own principles and today abides by them only selectively. What were once double standards are now in many cases triple or even quadruple standards. Thus Westerners fail to understand why these rights, unquestionably universal in their eyes, are not yet universally perceived as such. They wallow in their indignation. We would be better off listening to people like the Iranian philosopher Ramin Jahanbeglou or the Russian writer Alexander Solzhenitsyn, who argue that universalism must not be founded on Western values alone.

The dangerously naïve concept of imposed democratization is a product of such parochialism. The triumphalism of the 1990s led many in the West to start believing in the process of democratization as an experience akin to that of Saint Paul: nonbelievers see the light (after a jarring fall) and are converted. Thus in

2003 Americans believed that democracy would rise from the ashes of Saddam Hussein's regime just as in 1979 Jimmy Carter expected it to emerge from the fall of the shah of Iran. Democracy would naturally follow tyranny, wouldn't it? But democracy has never taken hold instantly, or completely, in any Western country, not even in the United States. Have we forgotten the extermination of the Indians, slavery, the Civil War, and racial segregation, let alone current problems like high rates of voter abstention, the role of money in elections, lobbies, and the Hollywoodization of politics (admittedly less and less particular to the United States). And in Europe, what about the centuries of bloody revolutions and vicious repression? In France, have we forgotten the 150 years between the first elections in 1795 and the right to vote for women?

Democracy has never been imposed from the outside as if by Martians. Ramin Jahanbeglou, who was imprisoned in Iran for his human rights activism, argues that the West should seek to promote it without seeking to impose it. Whenever France—whether in its revolutionary, imperial, or colonial phase—has tried to impose its principles, the effort has backfired. Democracy everywhere is the fruit of a complex process that moves at different speeds, sometimes forward, sometimes backward, with internal and external dynamics, but always essentially endogenously. When, during one of our long and friendly conversations, I said to Madeleine Albright that "democracy is not like instant coffee," I was unwittingly using a notion formulated by the Mexican writer

Octavio Paz, who said that democracy was "not Nescafé." How could we confuse the *reestablishment* of democracy (after 1945 in Germany, Italy, Spain, Portugal, Greece, and some Latin American countries) with the effort to *establish* democracy in places where it had never taken root (in Iraq in 2003 and Afghanistan in 2002)? How could we compare homogeneous populations (like Japan's) with heterogeneous ones (like Iraq's or Nigeria's)? How could we not see the difference between easily exportable democratic techniques (such as monitored elections) and aspects of democratic culture (such as respect for minority and individual rights) that take years to take root? In short, how could we confuse autonomous democratization specific to each society and democratization imposed from the outside? The idea of imposing democracy from the outside is even more absurd when it's being done by former colonial powers or by an America that has lost legitimacy in the eyes of much of the world.

Consider everything that Westerners—Americans and Europeans alike—have tried to do in the name of democratization in terms of declarations, speeches, sanctions, and conditionality toward the Russians, Chinese, Arabs, Africans, and others, and then measure the meager results. And further consider the fruits of such efforts implemented through war. It's enough to make one think that seeking to export our democratic regimes at all costs almost inevitably produces the opposite of the desired goal. Unless, of course, the real—and deeply cynical—goal is to stall the rise of emerging powers. But that's a different issue. And besides, the apostles of democratization are generally sincere.

But Europeans (and Canadians) are misguided in ways that even most American Democrats are not, for example on the issue of international civil society. Although no one can really identify what international civil society consists of (voters, NGOs, the UN, the media?), Europeans and Canadians see in it the key to getting beyond the nation-state, a sort of panacea for achieving modernity. In the United States, by contrast, no one really questions the concept of national sovereignty.

Europeans see the UN and multilateralism not only as diplomatic tools for achieving compromise but also as a means to move beyond the nefarious concept of the national interest—or in European newspeak, "national selfishness." International law is supposed to deter war criminals from committing their heinous acts or, if not, at least put an end to their impunity. Beyond that, and more problematically, it's supposed to help resolve fundamental political issues—to perform miracles, in other words.

In the eyes of the well-meaning Left, managed globalization is an oxymoron. To them, globalization cannot be managed because it is by definition chaotic. And the French harbor their own particular illusions: the idea of a powerful Europe and the related notion, dear to former president Jacques Chirac, of a "multipolar world." One of the "poles" would of course be Europe, led by France, and so the idea is seen in France as a sort of substitute for French power. The multipolar world would constrain American power. In the real world, however, the kind of multipolar world emerging suddenly before our eyes looks nothing like France's comforting vision.

In fact, neither American hubris (what's left of it after Iraq), nor European sincerity, nor French idealism and grandiloquence serve us well. Neither America's enormous power nor Europe's earnestness in seeking to strengthen international law and establish European norms is having the desired effect. Even worse, in our media-dominated societies, in which people spend on average three and one-half hours per day watching television, it is increasingly difficult to conduct a serious and coherent foreign policy focused on the long term. Our societies insist on "transparency" and "proximity" to power. People are constantly bombarded with new information and are skeptical of their leaders and the information they are given. Foreign policy suffers when it's based on superficial or unrealistic analysis and held hostage to domestic politics and constantly changing public opinion.

We've seen this all coming for some time now, but it keeps getting worse. Henry Kissinger used to complain that Israel was weakened by having only domestic politics and no foreign policy. Isn't that more or less the case with our media-obsessed democracies today?

All this high-minded Western universalism is well-meaning, but it is also arrogant, unrealistic, and paternalistic. It is a new form of *unrealpolitik* that is now running up against the reality of seemingly intractable divisions. Those divisions were apparent, for example, in 1995, when an extremist Israeli killed the Middle East peace process by assassinating Yitzhak Rabin, the most courageous and far-sighted Israeli leader of the past several decades. Rabin, who cannot be praised enough, used to say that he would "fight terrorism as if there were no peace process" but also that he would "pursue the peace process as if there were no terrorism." This allowed him to deny the terrorists the ability to control events. To be sure, after Rabin's death, the peace process launched by the first President Bush and James Baker staggered on for a while, only to crumble altogether after the election of Benjamin Netanyahu in 1996. Since then, there has barely been any hope for a lasting peace, except briefly in 2000, the year of missed opportunities. And this open wound poisons the entire relationship between the West and the Islamic world.

The notion that people are inevitably converging toward global consensus is also contradicted by the resurgence of intercommunal or ethnic conflicts—for example in the Balkans, the Caucasus, Rwanda, India, and the Muslim world. Thus the weeklong UN World Conference against Racism (a seemingly consensual issue if there ever was one) in Durban, South Africa, which ended on September 7, 2001, failed over the issue of how to treat the history of slavery and its political consequences. The failure was a brutal reminder—to the optimists who needed it—of the huge gap on this issue between the West on one hand and Africans and Muslims on the other.

When George W. Bush became the forty-third president of the United States in January 2001, he took office with a view of domestic and international policies that stupefied and frightened Europeans. They thought these ideas were outmoded, even though

Europe itself is no more than a protected little island in today's world. The September 11, 2001, terrorist attacks, however, demonstrated spectacularly that in a globalized world, terrorism is also global. The attacks were particularly stunning because they were perpetrated against American citizens, who thought—along with the rest of the world—that America was invulnerable. But it turned out that even the hyperpower was vulnerable to suicide attacks.

September 11 is not the dividing line between the old world and the new that many suggest. It is not of comparable importance to the fall of the Berlin Wall. But September 11 did give Vice President Dick Cheney and the neoconservatives the pretext they needed to engineer a reorientation of the Bush administration's foreign policy. That policy was already Manichaean, but now it would become even more missionary, military, and interventionist. Iraq made the ideal target because it was unable to defend itself and its regime was indefensible. The case for war was built on mendacious arguments and on the desire to demonstrate American power. The reasons included American pride, energy strategy, support for Israel, and the promotion of democracy. French President Jacques Chirac's vehement opposition and clear warnings about the mess that would follow an invasion could not change American minds. That only happened once the Americans realized they had made a mistake. They did not, however, necessarily realize the link between that mistake and the fundamental premises that led to it.

On the European side, political and economic integration had advanced rapidly in the late 1980s and early 1990s under the leadership of François Mitterrand, Helmut Kohl, and Jacques Delors. With impressive foresight, they began to prepare for the end of the bipolar era in the best possible way, by reinforcing Europe—a process they pursued right up until the 1992 ratification of the Maastricht treaty, which created the European Union (EU). The process moved forward again when eleven countries adopted the euro as their common currency on January 1, 1999, and in successive stages as fifteen more countries became EU members over the next eight years. On the institutional level, however, the federalists' attempt to leap ahead in the 2001 Nice treaty—supported by Germany to increase its weight in EU institutions and by France for less understandable reasons—led to a dead end with the demise of the 2004 Treaty establishing a Constitution for Europe, or constitutional treaty. That agreement was rejected by 54.7 percent of the French on May 29, 2005, and by 61.6 percent of the Dutch a few days later. In 2007, EU leaders tried again with a simplified treaty signed in Lisbon, but that treaty was also rejected in a referendum, this time in Ireland, in June 2008. In the wake of these setbacks, Europeans have seemed uncertain about what they want, which undermines the prospects of a multipolar world containing a strong European pole.

In fact, in 2008, after a decade of big UN summits, seven years after the spectacular adoption of the Millennium Declaration by the United Nations, and three years after the provisional agreement on the EU constitution, the world is no "community," and Europe is a long way from being a major power. To be sure, there's a community for finance ministers and foreign ministers from 192 countries, for the 120,000 bureaucrats who work for international organizations, and for thousands of NGOs from all over the world. And no doubt the world economy is globalized for lots of top executives, bankers, traders, pension fund managers, corporate lawyers, the media elite, proponents of "world food," the fashion industry, and the world of the high arts. But not for ordinary people. Except for this very thin, Americanized, and globalized veneer, we have not succeeded in building a community that brings the world's peoples together. Not only have we not yet arrived at Thomas Friedman's "flat" world, we might actually be moving in the opposite direction.

Many in the West thought that they already lived in an "international community" with common values, where people worked to meet the "challenges of the third millennium" according to modern, multilateral rules. A few remaining rogue states, according to this illusion, could be persuaded quickly to rejoin the liberal and democratic consensus. But the reality looks very different. It shows that the vagueness of the concept of an "international civil society" hides the same balance of power as exists in traditional international relations. China, for example, is brilliant at infiltrating international conferences with its so-called GONGOs—government-operated nongovernmental organizations. We must realize that this international civil society is represented by those who want to see it become more powerful. Of the world's 192 countries, nearly 130 have no NGOs at all. And the NGOs with the most resources and connections are Western, almost all of them American or British.

Where the economy is concerned, the world has certainly been "decompartmentalized" by the end of the East-West conflict and the falling of trade barriers. Increased trade has led to strong economic growth: from 1950 to 2003, international trade grew by an average of 6 percent a year and worldwide production by 4 percent. Since 1975, international trade has grown from 8 percent of world GDP to 20 percent. The world seems unified and harmonized by the instant distribution of images and information and the dramatic fall in the cost and time of transportation.

If we didn't have to worry about unresolved political issues or injustice, it would be easy to be optimistic. We could focus on the great prospects for world growth that result from the huge, unsatisfied needs of poor countries, the unlimited opportunities for mergers and acquisitions, capitalism's inexhaustible capacity to regenerate itself even as companies wage merciless war on each other, or the appetite of multinational firms in the West and the developing world, not to mention the gold mine represented by the opportunity to convert an ecologically destructive economy into an ecologically sustainable one. But that would be to look at the world with blinders on, because the world remains marked by staggering inequalities, deepening conflicts, deep resentments and misunderstandings, the desire for revenge, mutual fear, and ticking political time bombs.

These dividing lines do not lie between the "North" and the "South," terms that no longer mean anything. Rather, they lie between the rich and the poor. Overall, poverty is falling. But in some places—in the former Soviet Union, Africa, and some Latin

American countries—it has been aggravated for years by the massive liberalization blindly promoted by international financial institutions in the name of the "Washington Consensus." That term was coined in 1989 by the economist John Williamson to describe what the Nobel Prize–winning economist Joseph Stiglitz later called "market fanaticism." What is indisputable is that visible and measurable inequalities are growing. They are caused by the enormous accumulation of speculative revenues received by the "winners," whether they be countries, regions, companies, or individuals.

As François Morin explains in his book *Le nouveau mur de l'argent* (The new wall of money), there is a fundamental disconnect between the real economy and the financial sphere. In 2002, the value of international trade in goods and services came to around $8 trillion, but the value of financial transactions was over $1,150 trillion—far more than the foreign reserves of all the central banks in the world put together. All these transactions take place with little transparency and are made by a relatively small number of traders and managers of hedge funds and pension funds—four-fifths of whom are registered in tax havens—and by sovereign wealth funds.

Within ten years of having invented a supposedly magic formula—the unregulated application of derivatives to an ever-increasing range of financial instruments—even the inventors of that formula came to realize that it was a fantasy. The 2007–08 financial crisis demonstrated that there's no such thing as an economy on autopilot. This sort of casino capitalism has led to enormous growth among the world's richest 2 percent, who own 50 percent of the world's assets, whereas the poorest 50 percent of people own just 1 percent of the assets. At the same time, according to the Millennium Declaration and the UN's World Food Program, 1 billion human beings live in "abject and dehumanizing conditions of extreme poverty," and 854 million are undernourished (consuming less than 1,900 calories per day). Thirty-four million of these very poor people live in rich countries.

Globalization fanatics think they can deal with these huge inequalities through the market, in which young and innovative entrepreneurs cleverly take advantage of price differentials between two continents—on Friedman's supposedly "flat" earth. But they see individuals as nothing more than undifferentiated consumers of goods and services, rather than as members of a political community rooted in a particular culture. The defenders of free trade always focus on the benefits to the consumer but never on what people lose in terms of democracy when the market rules. And the environmental degradation caused by this form of globalization is rarely taken into account by free marketeers. At least some economists are now starting to pay attention: a report by Lord Stern in the United Kingdom concluded that in the absence of concerted action, global warming alone could reduce global GDP by up to 20 percent. Avoiding the worst effects of climate change will cost at least 1 percent of GDP, or around $6 trillion.

There's also an enormous gap between countries that are relatively well protected from major environmental threats and those that, in contrast, are more exposed to them. According to Al Gore, in *An Inconvenient Truth,* in the more vulnerable countries some 200 million environmental refugees could be driven from their homes by rising water levels. Many countries also remain unprotected against health threats from dangerous chemicals, unlike Europe, which is covered by the European Commission's REACH program (Registration, Evaluation, Authorization, and Restriction of Chemical substances). And in many countries nothing is done to prevent shortages of clean air, clean drinking water, farmland, livable areas, forests, silence, space, and beauty.

Then there's the gap between the relatively secure and settled populations of the thirty richest countries and the world's 175 million refugees (3 percent of the world's population) who move around year by year, and sometimes, at the end of their long and dangerous journeys, are exploited or forced into hiding.

Sadly, another division is the one separating various civilizations, even if we deny this reality because it scares us. To be sure, only small minorities within these civilizations actually seek confrontation—out of ignorance or fanaticism. In the Muslim world, the clash is between two opposing minorities, religious fundamentalists and moderate modernists, who are struggling to win over the much larger masses. Of course, the lack of education has a lot to do with it. But we've got to admit that this clash of ignorance, prejudice, misunderstanding, and mutual fear risks becoming a true Islamic-Western "clash of civilizations," an extension of the clash within the Islamic world between modernists and fundamentalists. These tensions, moreover, are exacerbated by irrational Western fears of Arabs and even Islam in general, by some

Islamists' desire to take revenge for the crusades or Western imperialism, and by the Arab-Israeli conflict. And we must also admit that the extremists are managing to attract sympathy and support even from beyond their traditional followers. Thus we see an Islam seized with fervor and self-affirmation in reaction to forced Westernization and to numerous failures. In Western countries, on the other hand, secularist activists, feminists, and human rights advocates clamor to put an end once and for all to this "Islamo-fascism," inevitably linked in their eyes to terrorism.

Nor must we forget, under this same heading, the world's many other divisions, like Islam/China, Islam/Hinduism, Islam/Orthodoxy, China/India, and Latin America/Andes/Iberia. The universal power and influence of these divisions should make us think twice about what to do about them rather than just reject the notion of a clash of civilizations out of hand.

Finally, we need to consider the striking divisions everywhere between the powerful and the vulnerable. In the first group are the American hyperpower, other rich countries, and emerging countries like China, India, Brazil, South Africa, and Vietnam. In the second group are dozens of the least-developed countries and failed or disintegrating states.

How are Westerners reacting to all this resistance, which contradicts their worldview, interferes with their policies, and will soon threaten their interests? Broadly, they waver between a hard-line and a softer approach, but on the whole they do not doubt the superiority of their values and interests, and very few accept a fundamentally realistic approach.

We must make a distinction here, however, between the economic world, whether in America or in Europe, and other areas. Business people, given the field they're in, have to be realistic. They see the world economy as it is today; otherwise they would fail miserably. So they figure out what's really going on, take a close look at what's changing, and act according to their interests. Thus is the world economy constantly adapting and expanding its hegemony thanks to the mechanism of globalization. Meanwhile, an unconstrained and permanent competition is taking place between Western styles of capitalism just like that between the West and the emerging countries. The main victim of this conflict could be the European social welfare system. Globalization pays no heed to the human, cultural, and political realities that get in its way.

Cultural, social, and political actors, on the other hand, are able to see the world however they want, without reality ever setting in. They project their conceptions on the rest of the world and wallow indefinitely in a media-driven narcissism without ever having to pay the price for their idealism. It's their countries that are paying the price.

Shocked by the fall in their popularity around the world, the Americans initially refused to change.[1] They intransigently

---

1. According to the Pew Research Center, between 2000 and 2006 those with a favorable view of the United States fell from 83 percent to 56 percent in the United Kingdom, 62 percent to 39 percent in France, 78 percent to 37 percent in Germany, 52 percent to 12 percent in Turkey, and 75 percent to 30 percent in Indonesia.

reasserted their values, preeminence, and exceptionalism, and they reaffirmed their right to wage preventive wars if their security so required. This hard-line view, which rules out the possibility of giving up the Western monopoly over world affairs, is held not only by American neoconservatives but also by many Europeans, although the latter rarely admit it. This ill-informed approach consists of thinking in terms of a "Western bloc," in particular vis-à-vis the Islamic world, Russia, and China. It means refusing to show flexibility and—in the case of the United States, as Zbigniew Brzezinski has pointed out—always wanting greater security than others. It means going on the offensive to promote our democratic "values" and defending human rights. It means keeping all options—including the offensive use of military force—on the table. This approach leads some to refuse to rule out the idea of turning NATO into an armed "alliance of democracies" by enlarging it to Ukraine and Georgia, or even to Japan, Australia, South Korea, and Israel, and by getting it involved—with hardly any debate—outside of its traditional zone of operations, as it has in Afghanistan.

But this approach is running up against certain realities. There are strategic realities, for example. After the Republicans were routed in the 2006 midterm congressional elections, mostly due to the Iraq fiasco, President Bush felt obliged to suggest that he was ready to be pragmatic and open to suggestions on what to do. But the Democrats, who almost all voted for the Iraq war, have no alternative policy.

There are also economic realities. New players, including emerging countries and global companies based in places like India, China, Brazil, and South Africa, are starting to change the meaning of a globalization that was supposed to consolidate Western hegemony, not challenge it. In 2007, the Boston Consulting Group's annual list of the top 100 companies from emerging economies included 41 from China, 20 from India, 13 from Brazil, 7 from Mexico, and 6 from Russia. Already, emerging countries are responsible for 15 percent of global mergers and acquisitions and 37 percent of all foreign investment. Such developments are making Westerners nervous. Americans are very worried about the growth of Chinese exports. Despite decades of bitter domestic conflict over the issue, official U.S. support for free trade had remained solid, thereby changing the world. Today that official support is eroding. Representatives and Senators from industrial states threatened by trade have begun to call for protectionist measures, yet to be adopted given the continued support for free trade—at least for the United States—among Republicans and Clintonian Democrats. Americans are also petrified by the power China derives from its massive holding of Treasury bills— hundreds of billions of dollars' worth—though no one really knows what to do about it. Some Americans (like Bill Clinton) see China as a potential partner. Others (like George W. Bush) see it as a strategic competitor. And still others (NGOs and the media) see it as a target for the promotion of human rights. In practice Washington treats China like all three at the same time.

As for Europe, its citizens are more worried now than at any time since the end of the cold war. Europeans see that the world has not become the "community" they had hoped for. Their reaction is somewhat contradictory. They follow a soft and ill-defined line seeking greater security but at the same time reasserting their "values" and hoping that their "soft power" will suffice. They think they can manage by asserting their desire to put morality at the heart of their foreign policy, thus protecting themselves from any old or new threats. This morality does not, however, extend to the point of refusing to sell Airbus planes to China or to purchase oil from the Arabs or natural gas from the Russians. But the combination of these principles is an odd one, reminiscent of the Kantian moralists once criticized by the French writer Charles Péguy: "Their hands are clean, because they have no hands." This contradiction gives European publics and elites an uncomfortable feeling of disarray.

Westerners today see themselves sitting atop Mount Olympus and believe more than ever in their alleged "mission" to run the world. But if they refuse to accept that they have lost their monopoly over world history—Westerners make up only around one billion of the world's six and one-half billion people, after all—they will find it increasingly difficult to realize their goals or even defend their interests.

An alternative approach is possible. It would consist of following a firm but realistic course—figuring out what Western interests are and negotiating as well as possible, both directly and at the UN and other international organizations, with the newly emerging powers and everyone else. That is the approach already taken at the World Trade Organization. If Westerners do that, and start making use of all aspects of foreign policy, they will be able to preserve immense long-term influence, especially if they learn to use it intelligently. In the fall of 2006, the Iraq Study Group, directed by James Baker and Lee Hamilton, proposed this sort of realist course. The administration rejected it out of hand even as Secretary of State Condoleezza Rice seemed in some ways to take inspiration from it.

All this makes the U.S. elections of 2008 particularly important—both for Americans and the world at large. Have Americans understood the real reasons for the failures of the Bush administration in the Middle East? Will they learn not to try to fight what Philip Gordon, in his 2007 book *Winning the Right War,* has called "the wrong war"? Will they manage to formulate policies that will defend, firmly and effectively but realistically, their interests and the interests of the West vis-à-vis emerging, reemerging, or already emerged powers? Will they treat their allies like responsible partners, and will they manage to be responsible themselves?

We can only hope so.

CHAPTER TWO

How to Build a Better World

Deploring political naïveté does not mean abandoning the goal of building a better world. On the contrary, it's a necessary step toward that goal.

Ideally, the world would follow the guidelines outlined in so many UN and Group of 8 (G-8) communiqués. Human rights would be respected, and men and women everywhere would find personal fulfillment. Everyone would belong to a single community where no one faced discrimination or mistreatment. People would join together to face common challenges like ending poverty, solving global warming, improving human health, ending shortages of clean air and water, preventing pandemic disease, managing migration, preventing the proliferation of weapons of mass destruction, stopping organized crime, ensuring cultural diversity, combating terrorism, and avoiding a clash of civilizations.

Aside from those who seek to establish the domination of one particular state or people over others, who does not support such lofty goals?

The nineteenth and twentieth centuries, especially in Europe, were marked by ideological struggles on which humanity's future depended. Some of these ideologies—which stood in for religions—turned out to be totalitarian in nature. They led to widespread famine, war, concentration camps, and mass killings. More than sixty years after World War II, more than thirty years after Deng Xiaoping's embrace of capitalism in China, and nearly twenty years after the fall of the Berlin Wall, what is left of this ideological clash?

The dominant, and almost exclusive, ideology remaining today is market capitalism. Its proponents claim that no other economic system in human history has ever been able to produce so many goods and services capable of meeting human needs. That happens to be true, but it's far from the whole story.

Dogmatic neoliberals even argue that the market economy is the only reliable way to determine what is good or bad for society. They apply this thinking to both the short term and the long term and to all areas well beyond economics. But the deregulated, speculative, and financial type of capitalism that has evolved over the past twenty-five years no longer resembles the mixed economy, the "Rhineland capitalism" practiced in France or Germany, or even the theory of the market economy. This new economy, after all, ensures its profitability by forcing society to bear the bulk of its social, human, and environmental costs. Moreover, it runs a very high risk of crisis when speculative bubbles burst. The American economist Joseph Stiglitz and the French economist Jean Peyrelevade are only two of the many experts who have warned about these excesses. The subprime crisis that began in the summer of 2007, and the chain reaction it has caused, should not have come as a surprise.

Even aside from the current crisis, if all these external costs appeared on the balance sheets of companies today, the concept of their "profitability" would be completely different. In that case, the market would be a more accurate indicator of sustainable growth. But we're not there yet. The ultra-free-market movement launched by Milton Friedman and propagated globally by Margaret Thatcher and Ronald Reagan has put proponents of state intervention, and even supporters of modest regulation, on the defensive. The movement is unlikely to fade anytime soon given the support for it in the developing world, not least in Asia. That's the story of global liberalization over the past fifteen to twenty years. It began with the fall of the Soviet Union and then moved on to the transformation of the General Agreement on Tariffs and Trade (GATT) into the World Trade Organization (WTO) in 1995; the steady expansion of the WTO's membership, reaching 150 with the accession of Vietnam in 2006; constant pressure to cut trade barriers; much faster growth of international trade than of productivity; and, most stunningly of all, the spectacular growth in the use of derivatives.

This tendency to allow market forces alone to govern world affairs is also leading to growing frustration and major resistance on several levels. Americans believe in the market but they also believe in American leadership. Europeans believe in the market, but they believe even more strongly in a more just and equal world, which is being undermined by globalization. A growing number of people in Europe, Latin America, Africa, and even the United States are in fact starting to realize that globalization has social, environmental, and political costs that can be greater than the wealth it creates. Average people in the West, in contrast to their elites, are skeptical about globalization; they see more disadvantages than advantages in it. According to the *Financial Times,* in July 2007 only 36 percent of Germans, 25 percent of Italians, 18 percent of French, 17 percent of Americans, 17 percent of Spanish, and 15 percent of Britons had a favorable view of globalization. In 2002, according to the Pew Research Center, 78 percent of Americans believed that "trade with other countries is a good thing for their country," but only 59 percent felt that way in 2007. In early 2008, moreover, the two leading candidates for the Democratic nomination for president pledged to renegotiate the North American Free Trade Agreement (NAFTA). The financial and economic crisis that began in the summer of 2007 and spread in 2008 could raise further questions about globalization. It could reopen the debate about the rules that should govern capitalism, about the role of states, and thereby about the role of multilateralism.

Where could all this lead? Left-wing groups around the world—and admittedly there are enormous differences among them, from northern European social-democratic movements to antiglobalization protesters and French socialists—all seek to promote greater equality and justice around the world. We must, however, distinguish between two groups. The first group rejects the very basis of the market economy on social, environmental, or philosophical grounds. It calls for some as-yet undefined alternative (given that the only known alternative, a planned economy, has already failed). The second group accepts the basic principles of the free market but wants to regulate it better, again in ways yet to be precisely defined.

The first group, the so-called *alter*globalization movement, questions the very principle of a market economy. Since it appeared in 1999 at the WTO summit in Seattle (when it was still known as the *anti*globalization movement), it has steadily evolved from more or less direct opposition to the market economy to the search for an alternative. At successive meetings in Porto Alegre, Genoa, and Davos (where the World Social Forum meets in opposition to the more famous World Economic Forum), this group has operated under the slogan "A better world is possible."

While hardly new, the arguments of the alterglobalization movement are worth serious consideration. Building on well-known critiques of capitalism, proponents of this view underscore the internal contradictions inherent in capitalism and denounce

the failure to take into account its social and environmental consequences. The logic of maximizing individual benefits, they
argue, leads to antagonism, rivalry, and conflict.

How can anyone fail to sympathize with these concerns? That
said, this diverse movement, split into factions with diverging
interests, is incapable of forming a clear alternative to global capitalism. Its "all or nothing" way of thinking all too often blinds it
to the capacity of the global economic system to evolve and
reform. The alterglobalization movement is simply not going to
succeed in limiting the unregulated global market economy's
tremendous power.

Perhaps that can be done by the second group, the supporters
of global economic regulation. This group accepts the idea of the
market economy but believes it can and must follow certain rules.
These rules apply at the level of the company (corporate governance), the state (a range of regulations), the European single market (rules for competition), and the international system (the
WTO). WTO Director General Pascal Lamy is a serious and sincere proponent of this line of thinking. He believes in the development of multilateral trade agreements and in greater cooperation among international institutions.

Nonetheless, the regulation that this group believes is necessary
is not so much regulation by the state as by supranational organizations acting independently of states. These regulators are trying
to put in place a set of international rules to govern globalization
that all political and economic entities, including states, are meant

to follow. And therein lies the problem: such an approach raises real questions about democracy. For example, the Multilateral Agreement on Investment developed by the OECD (Organization for Economic Cooperation and Development) would have taken important prerogatives away from the state and given them to companies. That's one reason why France's Socialist prime minister Lionel Jospin rejected it in 1999. States would have had to agree to submit unconditionally to international arbitration, which would have called into question an inalienable attribute of sovereignty—the right of jurisdiction.

The problem with this sort of "global governance" is that the rules generated by these expert panels and corporate police go well beyond the framework to which they're meant to apply—the market for goods and services. For example, competition law within the European Union (EU)—at least as interpreted by the European Commission's Directorate General for Competition and the European Court of Justice—increasingly influences the economies, societies, and corporate life of the member states. Similarly, the WTO Dispute Settlement Mechanism and other international trade agreements have an influence on international affairs that goes well beyond trade issues. Those who believe Montesquieu's idea that the natural effect of trade is to bring about peace take delight in such developments. They are thrilled with the hundreds of free trade agreements signed since GATT was founded. They see a beautiful future for all humanity in the growing role played by trade in the world economy, and they see catastrophe in the potential failure of the Doha Round. Indeed, the "international community" rushed to launch this latest trade round in 2001, right after the 9/11 terrorist attacks, to send a message that the terrorists would not win. As if the terrorists were protectionists!

Paradoxically, some alterglobalization activists and some partisans of the Washington Consensus seem to come together to flirt with the concept of "world government." One can only wonder how a concept with such an obvious potential for despotism manages to seduce anyone from the ranks of the antitotalitarian Left. What global government are they talking about? Designed by whom? To do what? Made up of whom? Controlled by whom? And if it becomes repressive, where on earth are its opponents to hide? Nobody asks these questions. Are they talking about a triumvirate made up of the UN Secretary General and the Directors General of the WTO and the International Monetary Fund (IMF)? Or perhaps the leaders of the Group of 8 (G-8), whom some misinformed alterglobalizationists—looking for something to protest against—paradoxically claim to see as the world's new governing board? Where does all this leave democracy?

World government, in any case, will not happen. The forces of deregulation that have been unleashed around the world are such that they cannot be controlled by any sort of global governance, or even by the American hyperpower. No person and no organization will ever control all that. Only the market is in charge, but that's the problem, because some theories notwithstanding, the market doesn't even control itself. And the market doesn't take into account that which it can't put a monetary value on, such as the long term or the general interest.

For many, the alternative to this line of thinking is multilateral cooperation among states, which has its own problems. Multilateralism is attractive to all those who want to improve the world without turning everything over to the market, those who are skeptical of world government, those who worry about the democratic deficit in global governance, and those who do not believe that a single country—even the United States—can take responsibility for world order. Thus the famous Millennium Declaration concludes with a chapter calling for the reinforcement of the UN and for more cooperation between the UN, IMF, the World Bank, and the WTO.

The lodestar of multilateralism is international cooperation in place of narrowly nationalist and unilateralist foreign policies. Such an approach began to appear even more attractive in the wake of the brutal and provocative unilateralism of the Bush administration's first years in power. In reality, however, multilateralism suffers from serious weaknesses. These are generally overlooked by its defenders in Europe and elsewhere, who tend to idealize the UN and its twenty-six organizations, commissions, and special conventions, as well as the Bretton Woods institutions (the IMF and the World Bank) and the WTO. According to multilateral principles, member states of the various organizations decide jointly, by unanimity or in some cases majority votes. The process is inevitably sluggish and unwieldy when these organizations have 150, 181, or 192 members, as with the WTO, IMF, and UN respectively (sovereignty has proliferated over the past forty years). The problem is appearing even within the EU, with its 27 members.

All this is well known. But what do Europeans usually propose to overcome these problems? They propose that states transfer or abandon even more of their sovereignty! That makes no sense. Most of these states have already been weakened by economic globalization, which they cannot control even if they have embraced it. But they've also been weakened because in the name of the Washington Consensus—or to please the markets and foreign investors—they have voluntarily given away many of the powers that they might have used to adapt to globalization. At least that is the case for most states, certainly the most naïve and easily influenced ones, but certainly not for the United States. On top of these difficulties is the pressure exerted by the media, public opinion, and NGOs, which can sometimes prod in a useful direction (for example on the issue of antipersonnel land mines) but which can also paralyze the system. The result of all this is that multilateralism becomes nothing more than a system for the weakening of states and the pooling of their weakness.

The paradox is that those who expect the most from the multilateral system—proregulation Europeans—have done the most to weaken its constituent parts: states. The initial impulse to reduce state power is easy to understand. It was obviously desirable to weaken not only totalitarian and repressive states but also sclerotic, bureaucratic states. Reformers have sought to regulate state power in a framework of the rule of law and to liberalize it via the free market. Today, however, with a few important exceptions, the world is suffering more from the weakness of states than from their excessive power. Developing countries need strong and capable democratic states, not just civil society and markets. If we don't do something about the weakness of states, people could come to see multilateralism as their only fallback: if nothing can any longer be done at the state level, as people keep saying, then no government is ever responsible for anything. Thus the growing gap between what is expected of the multilateral system and what it can actually produce. This gap produces one disappointment after another, which leads the states that are already skeptical of multilateralism to move even further away from it. The United States, which fits into this category, will only find more reasons to prefer "multilateralism à la carte"—working only with those states that agree to go along in "coalitions of the willing," such as the one put together for the Iraq war.

I have already noted some of multilateralism's big disappointments, such as the obviously unattainable objectives of the Millennium Declaration and the revealing failure to adopt the conclusions of the 2001 Durban World Conference against Racism. But there are plenty of others: the lack of any measurable benefits from the dozen or so big UN summits held over the past ten years; the lack of any real impact from unanimous Security

Council decisions since the one authorizing the 1991 Gulf War; the failure of the Doha trade round, launched in 2001 in the framework of the WTO; the decline of the IMF because it is no longer as necessary as it used to be (which could, of course, be a good thing); the inability of the IMF's managing director, Dominique Strauss-Kahn, to persuade countries of the North to transfer more than 1.6 percent of votes to countries of the South; the controversial nature of the World Bank's role and contradictory policies; the frequent struggle by members of the EU—all twenty-seven of them and counting—to agree; and the flouting of the Nuclear Non-Proliferation Treaty (NPT) by a number of countries. Enduring the unproductive meetings associated with all these efforts—reminiscent of dreadful and never-ending co-op owners' meetings—is enough to make anyone despair.

But we need not resign ourselves to the all-controlling, free-market "hyper-empire" described by Jacques Attali in his 2006 book *Une brève histoire de l'avenir* (*A Brief History of the Future*), in which states and territorial democracies disappear. We must neither abandon the multilateral system nor create an ideological "community of democracies," which would certainly complete the process of turning the UN into the League of Nations. On the contrary, we must relegitimize the multilateral system and make it more effective. And that process requires the rehabilitation of states.

ᥱᥩ ᥱᥩ ᥱᥩ

Reforming and relegitimizing the UN is no easy task, as is clear from the countless reports and proposals for reform that have had little effect. We must remember that in 1919 and in 1945, the winners dictated the terms and the content of the charters of the League of Nations and the United Nations. Even though the UN charter begins with the pompous "We the Peoples of the United Nations," the fact is that it was mostly written by lawyers from the U.S. State Department before others were given a modest role in its negotiation.[1] This process is rather different from the one required today to amend the charter—the agreement of all five permanent members of the Security Council (still the United States, Russia, China, the United Kingdom, and France) and of two-thirds of the 192 members of the General Assembly. Although there was certainly a winner and a loser following the cold war, there was not in 1991–92 a "postwar" period in the same way as after 1945, with the Potsdam, San Francisco, and Bretton Woods conferences. Russia, like the United States and the other permanent members, has maintained its veto right and is reestablishing its influence.

Kofi Annan, UN secretary general from 1997 to 2006, was therefore right to try to reform the main UN institutions, starting

1. The rest of the preamble goes on to claim the resolve "to save succeeding generations from the scourge of war, which twice in our lifetime has brought untold sorrow to mankind . . . to practice tolerance and live together in peace with one another as good neighbors."

with the Security Council. Even while doing so, there was no point in trying to end the status of the permanent members or eliminating the veto right, for two reasons. The first was that these features were adopted in the UN charter in part to compensate for the failure of the League of Nations, whose lack of a strong Security Council contributed to its ineffectiveness. The second was that if there were no Security Council and no veto right, the key current permanent members would simply quit the UN. As for the idea of a common European seat for the twenty-seven EU members, it would have the practical effect of replacing the British and French ambassadors with an EU representative who would have to abstain nine times out of ten because the EU couldn't reach a decision in time. And this will be the case for a long time to come.

Putting aside these unrealistic solutions, it should be possible to move forward in one of two ways. One would be to create five or six new permanent members with a veto right (Japan, India, Germany, a Latin American country, an African country, and an Arab country, with a rotating representative from the region in the latter three cases). I believe this could be agreed to despite the opposition of some of the current Security Council members and of some jealous neighbors of the candidates. The other option would be to bring in new permanent members without the veto right—if they agreed to join on that basis. It is of course also possible to create new nonpermanent members, as proposed by a UN advisory committee in 2004, but that would be just a stopgap.

Another option would be to limit the veto right, for example by requiring two or three vetoes on certain subjects, or limiting the length of time a veto would be valid. To find a balance between sovereignty and the necessity of preventing a humanitarian crisis, I have previously suggested that the use of vetoes could be suspended for a limited time (three to six months, renewable once or twice) to aid a population deemed by an international body of respected experts to be in imminent danger. The UN managed to reach a compromise on the issue of the "responsibility to protect." But we always end up in the same place: no reform is possible unless the permanent members all agree, and yet several permanent members are dead set against such significant change. We must nonetheless continue to develop, promote, and defend UN reform proposals in anticipation of the day when a new U.S. political context (a new Roosevelt? a new Clinton?) makes it possible to implement them. Until that day, we must continue to work to raise the costs to Russia, China, and yes, even the United States for opposing such obviously necessary reforms.

Other UN reforms are also desirable. The UN Human Rights Commission, which had lost all credibility, was partly reformed in 2005 (when it became the Human Rights Council) but is now not much better than its predecessor. It may be that the very concept of a UN human rights organization is the problem. Should the UN even have such a group when its rules mean that the members of that group will hardly be model human rights performers? On the other hand, the elevation of the Economic and Social Council could empower it to arbitrate and harmonize major decisions not only on areas like trade but also on labor laws and the environment, working with the WTO, the International Labor Organization (ILO), and a World Environment Organization yet to be created. The reactivation of the UN Trusteeship Council, responsible for temporarily supervising failed states, would make it possible to avoid relying on the closest regional power. In 2004 France's then agriculture minister, Henri Nallet, and I also proposed a "Global Consultative Council for Civil Society," which would meet every year to petition and ask questions of the General Assembly. Who would belong to such a group, given that some NGOs are highly credible, others are somewhat credible, and some are not credible at all? All multilateral institutions have developed various criteria for representation. It should be possible to find the right balance.

For a number of years already, some Europeans and leftist movements worldwide have been calling for the creation of a World Environment Organization (WEO) or a United Nations Environment Organization (UNEO). France has been pushing for something along those lines ever since the 1992 UN Conference on Environment and Development, in Rio de Janeiro. The details have not been fleshed out, but its functions could include providing a forum for negotiations on the full range of environmental issues; serving as a clear and credible interlocutor for the other international institutions (IMF, World Bank, WTO) as they try to implement the more than 500 existing regional or bilateral environmental agreements; controlling sufficient resources and expertise to oversee the application of various multilateral agreements (like the Kyoto accord and others); and taking over the activities of the UN Environment Program and the Global Environmental Fund (such as oversight and training for developing countries) and other specialized conventions. Naturally, all this must be done without creating a stifling bureaucracy.

In the nuclear field, the most urgent priority is to relegitimize the Treaty on the Non-Proliferation of Nuclear Weapons (NPT). Doing so requires dealing with the countries that do not really respect its rules, such as North Korea and Iran, and with nonsignatories who have nuclear weapons, such as Israel, India, and Pakistan. It also means clarifying the conditions in which countries can transfer technology and provide assistance for the development of civil nuclear programs. In short, it is necessary to recreate a consensus around a more realistic treaty that promotes civil nuclear development while deterring its military counterpart and which could form the basis for discussion at the next NPT Review Conference, in 2010. New progress toward nuclear disarmament, and specifically nuclear reductions by the two countries that possess 95 percent of the world's nuclear warheads—the United States and Russia—would be a major contribution. And you don't have to believe in the utopian idea of a denuclearized world to support such a goal.

All these reforms would make the multilateral system more legitimate and effective. They would also make it possible to pursue an alternative (the only possible alternative, in fact) to the growing tendency to want to create a "Western bloc" based on allegedly universal values designed to protect against the threat of a barbarous world. Faced with the loss of their monopoly over world affairs, this is the defensive posture adopted by certain Western elites and a position I described in a report for French President Nicolas Sarkozy as "Occidentalist." A not-so-distant cousin of American neoconservatism, Occidentalism seeks to spread and transform NATO radically in the absence of any serious debate. It would turn this once defensive "North Atlantic" alliance, eventually expanded to include Japan, Australia, and Israel among others, into the military arm of global democracy. Its mission would be to act well beyond its original geographic zone—as it is already doing in Afghanistan—under the pretext of fighting terrorism or defending our values. But have we really thought through just where such an approach to global challenges leads?

A new kind of multilateralism could also be the best way for the United States to recover its faltering position as a world leader. U.S.-China relations are increasingly strained. India is rising as a regional power. Latin America is distancing itself from its big northern neighbor. American domination is increasingly resented, including among its allies like South Korea and Japan, and, in the Arab world, violently rejected. (This rejection may be the only thing that holds the "Arab street" together amidst all the national divisions.) In short, America is facing a huge challenge of restoring its image—no longer the "land of the free and the home of the brave" in the minds of migrants from all over the world. After eight years of the Bush administration, will Americans admit this in 2009? I certainly hope so.

Still, we must be clear: apart from delegating certain competencies, multilateral organizations cannot and must not substitute for governments and states. The European Union is a special case, but in general, multilateral organizations have no specific personality. They constitute the framework in which governments negotiate and agree on a certain position, program, or course of action, but they are not meant to be the place for these same governments to abdicate their role or ignore their responsibilities.

Why make such obvious points? Because many Europeans naïvely see the multilateral system as a self-standing entity that can substitute for states, a sort of supranational appeals court where self-centered states can be kept in check. In fact, the multilateral system is nothing but the assemblage of states—it's all of us together. The directors of international organizations and their teams cannot do very much without very quickly running up against a problem of legitimacy. Similarly, the expression "international architecture" is misleading. There is certainly no "architect," and if there's any architecture it's pretty baroque. There's no central brain secretly organizing the multilateral system.

The gap between what many expect of multilateral organizations and the reality is constant, visible, and demoralizing. The legitimacy of those organizations is thus in question. The G-7, now the G-8, has no official basis but derives its importance

(which is in any case exaggerated by the media and alterglobalization activists) from the practice of annually bringing together the
leaders of the big industrialized countries—except, of course,
India and China. Studies have considered what a true grouping
of leading nations would look like: it would be a combination of
an enlarged Security Council, an enlarged G-8, and the IMF's
International Monetary and Financial Council (formerly the
Interim Committee). The result would be what former European
Commission president Jacques Delors once called an "Economic
and Security Council." Somewhere between the current situa-
tion and that kind of group is the idea of a G-13, relaunched by
French president Nicolas Sarkozy and British prime minister
Gordon Brown.

Fond of slogans, the French for a long time put their hopes in
the concept of a "multipolar world," though they never really
defined its composition, the relationship between the poles, or
how it would fit with the multilateral system. The idea was that
France would have an appropriately grand role in this multipolar
world, escaping the oppressive unipolar American system yet
somehow avoiding the paralyzing constraints of the multilateral
system. Paris would, in this scheme, exercise disproportionate
influence as part of a strong European "pole." But this line of
thinking doesn't really serve France well when French influence
has taken a beating in a weak Europe and when Europe is not a
major player in the multipolar world. This is especially true when
nothing guarantees the stability of the system, which could end up

as a sort of "balance of poles" like the old "balance of power," with constantly changing alliances and "interpolar" war. We must also clarify whether this multipolar world is (1) something that already exists and is merely being taken note of in the wake of developments like the rise of China (which is how French president Chirac saw it) or (2) on the contrary, an objective we're trying to promote through the inclusion of Brazil, Russia, India, China, South Africa, and others. Seeking such a goal would seem to be a sign of aggressiveness toward the Americans, who hate the concept. Either way, a multipolar world would have to be institutionalized somehow. In the meantime, the rapid development of direct relations among Central Asia, East Asia, India, Latin America, the Middle East, and Africa—for energy or other reasons—is striking. Neither the United States nor Europe has anything to do with these relationships. That particular multipolar world was not made by the West. Indeed it might even displace Europe.

What the European multilateralists and reformers must understand, in any case, is that the continued weakening and delegitimizing of states—a dominant stream of thinking for thirty years—is wrong; it will not lead to a better world. To see why, consider what must be done to meet the key global challenges we face:

—In the heart of the capitalist world, we find ourselves dealing with banks that are failing because of careless lending practices and a U.S. and global economic debacle resulting from the collapse of an elaborate system of high-risk debts. To deal with these challenges, we discover that we need governments and states.

—On the environment, the Kyoto treaty is nothing but the obligations that signatory states have accepted to satisfy the desires of their citizens. And who is going to ensure the application of the EU's REACH directive on dangerous chemicals if not the member governments of the EU?

—Where poverty is concerned, the UN World Food Program plays an indispensable role in managing emergency aid that feeds some 60 million people. But it is obvious that poverty can only really be reduced if rich countries cooperate in pursuing the right national development and growth policies.

—Governments must also manage migration, which is set to rise significantly in the coming decades. In a number of developing countries, the absence of states with the capacity to ensure security, social solidarity, and a feeling of national belonging is a much greater handicap than the bloated bureaucracies of those states that are so often criticized. Civil society is not a panacea.

—The fight against pandemic diseases is futile if the warnings of the World Health Organization are not efficiently relayed by well-organized states, determined governments, capable bureaucracies, and well-informed publics.

—Capable states are also necessary to fight against all aspects of the illegal economy. That economy includes the illicit drug trade (which, according to the UN, generates revenues of $500 billion per year), organized crime, human trafficking, and money laundering (which the IMF says amounts to between 2 and 5 percent of world GDP). Meeting this challenge requires national (or regional) police forces, customs officers, judges, and a range of government officials who are trained to work together.

—Many believe that the defense of cultural diversity and identity (including linguistic diversity) can be pursued with international legal exceptions to trade laws, so that national cultures are not leveled off under the steamroller of globalization. Such a defense is the goal of the Convention on the Protection and Promotion of the Diversity of Cultural Expressions, adopted by the 148 member states of UNESCO (UN Educational, Scientific and Cultural Organization) on October 20, 2005, on the basis of a French proposal. But it can be implemented only through the regulatory, legislative, and fiscal action of each government.

Preventing a "clash of civilizations" is a different kind of issue, but let me address it here because it also falls in the category of building a better world—or at least making this world less bad. Many of those who see in the phrase nothing but an irritating theory or a potentially self-fulfilling prophecy feel they need only rise in their ivory towers and denounce it as heresy to make it disappear as if by magic and to make people stop holding it up like a battle flag at bellicose rallies. Others think it can be beaten to death with "cultural dialogues," in which multilateral institutions are particularly adept.

But a different response is necessary for those like me who believe that the clash of civilizations is, unfortunately, a real threat. It's not enough to organize dialogues among tolerant—and unrepresentative—individuals from different parts of the world. What we need are political responses. Taking a political approach means not using military force and not refusing—as a matter of principle—to speak with certain interlocutors on the grounds that doing so will legitimize the illegitimate. Imagine where we'd be today if Nixon and Kissinger, instead of going to China in the middle of the cold war to see Mao—who threatened the West with nothing less than annihilation—had taken such an intransigent, pseudomoralistic position. The point of diplomacy is to make it possible to speak to your adversaries in the hope that you won't have to go to war with them. To act politically is to put out the fires that fuel the clash of civilizations. And how can that be done without states?

The Israeli-Palestinian conflict, the open wound that has poisoned relations between the West and the Arab and Muslim worlds for decades, cannot be resolved without the creation of a viable Palestinian state. That state would live side by side with the state of Israel, whose existence and borders would be recognized unambiguously by its neighbors and whose security would be guaranteed by the major powers, first and foremost the United States. The basic outlines of such a settlement are well known (the Clinton "parameters," the Taba negotiations, and the Geneva Initiative of Yasser Abed Rabbo and Yossi Beilin contain the main elements), and the Arab and Israeli publics want peace. "All" that's needed is for leaders and governments to muster the necessary courage and go all the way despite the obstacles and provocations. Individual initiatives from civil society will not suffice.

Apart from a few lunatics and two or three hostile states, the entire world will help those who demonstrate the necessary courage. It is significant that in the 2006 *Iraq Study Group Report,* co-chairs James Baker and Lee Hamilton argued that to cope with the deteriorating situation in the broader Middle East, the United States also had to reengage in the Israeli-Palestinian conflict. In Ramallah in January 2008, President Bush made a remarkable declaration given his policies to that point. He said it was an urgent necessity to end Israel's forty-year-old occupation of the West Bank and to create a Palestinian state whose map did not resemble Swiss cheese. If only he had pursued those goals during the previous seven years! In fact his administration's approach was the opposite of the Ramallah declaration, yet his 2008 declaration was not criticized by Israeli prime minister Olmert. As Henry Kissinger has said, the Arab-Israeli conflict is the only one in the world whose solution is known to all. Implementing it will require an Israeli prime minister strong and courageous enough to set it in motion and a Palestinian leader strong and courageous enough to sign and take responsibility for it.

გ გ გ

In speaking of states in this context, I am referring to capable, modern states that cooperate with one another, focus on their true tasks, and are engaged in a process of democratization—activities that are very different from those of bellicose states of years past.

We cannot transfer the necessary activities of the modern state to the "international community," the UN, or some other providential actor. Sovereignty abandoned by states is not transferred to the European or global level or to some new democratic space. If it's picked up at all, it is picked up by the market or by self-designated mechanisms that claim to be self-regulating but in reality are not. States therefore remain indispensable in their specific roles. Besides, as the French scholar Samy Cohen pointed out in 2003, they fight back. The former neoconservative Francis Fukuyama goes even further. In his 2004 book *State Building: Governance and World Order in the 21st Century*, he argues that states remain indispensable, but he remains skeptical—I think rightly so—about the possibility of building them from the outside.

There is still no such thing as an "international community" to build a better world. There is no celestial—or supranational—entity that can substitute for states. Not even the so-called "new actors" in international relations can do so. Only we can do it—192 states working together. No international community, no United Nations will act in our place, no market will focus on the long term. It is therefore time to break with this pessimistic, post-national line of thinking that for years has been positing the inevitable and even desirable decline of states. Such thinking has been shared by ideological liberals, speculators, former European leftists, Eurofederalists, and multilateral idealists; it has both exacerbated the ineffectiveness of the international system and led European integration into a dead end since 2005. The United

States has mostly been spared this illusion. Even for the most internationalist of Americans, participating in the international system means trying to influence it, not neglecting or discrediting it or giving in to it. Even the most multilateralist of Americans think in terms of U.S. leadership.

Even as they seek a new post-Iraq policy, a process accelerated by the presidential election campaign, the Americans do not share the Europeans' dangerous illusions. Rather, they confront the real and still valid choice outlined by Zbigniew Brzezinski: either seek to develop leadership or continue to pursue, in a different form, the dangerous and destabilizing policy of domination that they have conducted for nearly eight years.

We need to find a new arrangement, negotiated at a new conference along the lines of those held in San Francisco, Bretton Woods, and Havana. This new arrangement would consist of American leadership (minus the temptation to create a new league of democracies under America's control outside of the UN); a renovated multilateral system bringing together relegitimized states; and a multipolar world, embodied in the creation of a G-12 or G-13, a sort of amalgamation of the current G-8 and the UN Security Council.

CHAPTER THREE

A Europe That Knows What It Is and What It Wants

For decades now, Henry Kissinger's famous quip about there being no single phone number for Europe has been a convenient reference point for gloating Americans and regretful Europeans alike. Europeans could often have responded by pointing out that the United States has itself often been divided among three or four competing centers of power, but that would have been facile. In any case we might as well just admit it: there will be no "United States of Europe." There will be no Philadelphia-style constitutional convention, no equivalent of George Washington talking about how Europeans are "all alike" in a farewell address. As former European Commission president Jacques Delors has put it, Europe—or more specifically, the European Union (EU)—is and will remain not a "federation" but a "federation of nation-states." To be even more precise, it is a "confederation of nation-states" in the wider EU of twenty-seven or more members and a "federation of nation-states" in the euro zone. Years of experience have demonstrated that identities and states do not disappear.

Does this mean the end of the European project? No. It just means that the project will become more creative and realistic. Europeans have perhaps been too thin-skinned about Kissinger's comment. After all, it is less important to have unified representation than to have shared perspectives and policies. Who cares if Europe speaks with many voices if all of them say the same thing and Europeans all want to move in the same direction? In any case, you can't unify people against their will. You have to go about it in a different way. But Europeans who know who they are and agree on what they want will have considerable influence in the world, both as partners with the United States and on their own.

They can reach this goal by confronting the issues that still divide them. Except for a few marginal political parties, Europeans do not question what has been done in their name by American and European leaders for the past fifty years. What they fail to agree on is where to take the Europe-building process from here. Indeed, the European Union is nervously uncertain about three aspects of its future: its political nature, its borders, and its role in the world. These uncertainties will have to be resolved.

The Political Future

The first issue—how power is shared among EU member states and between those states and Brussels—has its roots in an uncertain period that began in the early 1990s, when member states felt they had to make a top priority of expansion to central and eastern Europe. Thus in 1996, the then fifteen members of the EU began a major negotiation to determine how many members of the European Parliament, how many members of the European Commission, and how many votes in the Council of the European Union the new member states would get. The meager results in the 1997 Amsterdam treaty led to a further negotiation at the Nice meeting of the European Council, which produced a new treaty signed in February 2001.

The Nice treaty was agreed to unanimously, but it was immediately criticized. Federalists complained that it did not make the necessary leap forward toward European integration. And Germany was frustrated by the fact that the "double-majority vote" (the requirement that a measure would need a majority both of states and population to pass) was not adopted. As a result, the idea began to take hold that a more ambitious treaty would have to be written. EU leaders thus agreed to hold a "European convention," designed to be more representative than a simple "intergovernmental conference" of heads of state and government because it would be made up of members of the European Parliament and national parliaments. Its mission would be to go further in the direction of political integration and to draft nothing less than a "constitutional treaty," which—for appearances' sake—would be called a "constitution." The result was the Treaty establishing a Constitution for Europe, signed in Rome in October 2004.

Legally, the name "constitution" was a lie, but it was thought to be a useful one. In fact it turned out to be counterproductive. The hubbub about the allegedly ambitious and radically new character of the "constitution" made it necessary for certain founding EU members—France and the Netherlands—to hold referendums. A referendum in France would clearly be risky, as the 1992 French referendum on the Maastricht treaty passed by less than a single percentage point. And the referendum campaign in France brought out all sorts of built-up contradictions and resentments. So some federalists voted for the treaty and denounced anyone who was against it, but other federalists voted no as a way of demanding more or different forms of integration. Many voted no for reasons having nothing to do with the treaty. Certain left-wing French and German leaders even called for a constituent assembly to "give power back to the people." "Europe," this loaded word, provoked all sorts of expectations and fears that had nothing to do with the treaty in question.

The confusion that reigned during the debate over the referendum in France had deep roots. It was the consequence of years of people carelessly saying things like "nothing can any longer be done at the national level" or "all that matters now is the European level," which had led people to blame Europe for all their problems. People began asking: If it's supposed to be a good thing that 60 percent of national legislation originates with the EU and that nation-states are being eroded by Europe, of what use is a national democracy like the French republic (or any other for that matter)?

Why even bother to have national elections? The result of all this was not surprising: an electoral insurrection against illegitimate political leaders, who became scapegoats for the public feeling of democratic denial.

To be fair, the most sincere and committed federalists had argued for a long time that democracy had to be strengthened at the European level—the only level that mattered in their eyes in relation to the United States, China, and other powers. They called for the creation of a new democratic space, including a European Parliament with expanded power that would monitor a reinforced European Commission built on a more political basis. In this vision, the European Council of heads of state and government would become a sort of Senate. This utopian and idealistic vision of Europe, which has affected the public and the media, nonetheless remains a minority view. But it raises serious questions. What language would this Europe speak? And who really accepts it? Not even Germany, despite the long-standing and common references there to the "United States of Europe" and "European federation." Who really believes that one day, even many years from now, European integration will turn Germany, France, Spain, and Sweden—let alone Great Britain— into regions like Bavaria, Scotland, or "Brittany"? Who thinks that France, Germany, and Spain will no longer exist in thirty years? Who could seriously compare Europe's ancient nations with even the oldest states in America? The European entity will remain unique.

In 2005, after 52 percent of the French and 56 percent of the Dutch voted no in their referendums on the constitutional treaty—the result of opponents who wanted more Europe, less Europe, or a different kind of Europe—EU leaders were bewildered. This rejection marked the end of the enlightened despotism that had guided European integration since 1950. But the supporters of the yes vote in France—pretty much the entire political class and the media—were unable to admit that the voters had dared vote against the direction of European history or, for that matter, against them. The elites were asking for confirmation from the electorate. And when they didn't get it they came closer than ever before in the modern era to denying democracy. Although the no vote was for the most part a reaction to a long-resented democratic deficit and not a vote against Europe itself, the elites could think of nothing but the need to vote again, to get around this mistake, to overcome France's "shame." They insisted that Europe would move forward without France despite the fact that all the essential issues are decided by unanimity. And anyway, where would Europe go? President Chirac was ridiculed for having taken the foolish risk of holding a referendum by the very critics who made that choice inevitable with their European maximalism and who had in any case demanded that he do so.

Eventually these twists and turns came to an end. Once elected president, Nicolas Sarkozy made the commitment that all European elites, particularly in Germany and Brussels, wanted the new French leader to make: no French referendum. In addition, he happily agreed to drop the notion of a European constitution and the symbols that went along with it, replacing them with a "simplified treaty."

The new treaty was agreed to in Lisbon in December 2007. Designed to replace the Nice treaty, it maintained the institutional provisions of the 2004 Rome "constitution," including the expansion of majority voting and, of course, the double-majority threshold. The Lisbon agreement was greeted with joy and relief. All but one of the EU member states agreed to begin the ratification process in 2008 without resorting to a referendum, the exception being Ireland, whose constitution required public approval of the treaty. But trouble appeared in June when 53 percent of referendum voters in Ireland rejected it.

However difficult will be the process of its adoption, the Lisbon treaty has the great advantage of bringing to an end ten years of sterile institutional controversies, in which Europeans fought over absurdities and federalists tried, yet again, to artificially create a European people from above. If there had been a constitutional treaty, would that not have been proof that there was, in fact, a "European people"? But that approach did not work, and it could not work. All this wasted time and energy could have been avoided with specific amendments to the Nice treaty after 2001. That would have also made it possible to adopt more common policies. No one today imagines that the twenty-seven will in the near future launch an uncertain negotiation of a more federalist treaty or that such a treaty could be ratified. The 2007

Lisbon treaty marked the most advanced possible point of political integration, even if some people still can't help but talk about possible new initiatives or stages of European integration. Perhaps the stabilization point for integration will have been the 2001 Nice treaty.

There are, no doubt, some well-meaning Americans who will regret Europe's inability to overcome its divisions. They will talk about steps in the right direction and, on their side of the Atlantic, maintain the same illusions as the remaining European federalists. Other, more numerous Americans will secretly rejoice over this European setback, which will reinforce their belief that the United States has no need to worry about European interference with its global leadership. But they may be mistaken because the harmonization of European policies could take other forms than the conventional ones the federalists sought to impose. In fact, the institutional clarification and stabilization provided by the Lisbon treaty should enable the twenty-seven to devote all their energy to the development of new policies and projects. Indeed, at this stage in its development, it is by freeing itself from the federalist dogma that Europe will be able to take concrete steps forward.

This line of reasoning remains valid after the Irish no. Perhaps, as they did after initially rejecting the Nice treaty, the Irish will re-vote and vote yes. But that's far from guaranteed. If Lisbon is not ratified, the EU will continue to work under the Nice treaty, which will not prevent it from coming up with new common policies or stronger cooperation among states.

What new policies should it focus on? The list of possibilities is long, and it goes beyond the permanent adoption of a common agricultural policy—which has been made all the more legitimate and pressing by the global food crisis—and the application of the Lisbon competitiveness programs. The priorities of the French EU presidency that started in July 2008 provide some good examples: an "immigration and asylum pact" to help control migration flows, a policy on energy and climate change, and the development of EU defense capabilities. All this will take years to implement. But common policies can also be pursued in other areas, like research, technology, and industry. They can involve all the member states; or just the euro zone; or a smaller, ad hoc group of states. They can be pursued via the community method—going through the commission and the parliament—or on an intergovernmental basis; there's no need to see the two approaches as incompatible. In a union of twenty-seven (and eventually more) members, it is obvious that not everyone will move ahead at the same speed. Remember that the 2004 constitutional treaty was a "framework treaty" that put in place a permanent negotiation in a number of different areas. We have to be flexible and willing to innovate. The Schengen open-borders process, for example, resulted from a very pragmatic approach, as did Ariane and Airbus, none of which have been integrated into the EU. The "Mediterranean Union"—a French project brought into the EU process at the last minute—could take the form both of reinforced cooperation within the EU and of a partnership with countries outside it.

The Lisbon treaty includes new elements that might allow for the expansion of community activity. The EU would have its own legal standing, which would enable it to sign certain international treaties in its own name. The European Parliament would join the Council of the European Union as a "colegislator" in an increased number of areas and would also elect the president of the European Commission. The Parliament would thus be increasingly powerful. The European Council, which is made up of the heads of the EU's member states, would have the same president for a renewable term of two and a half years (though he or she will also have to figure out how to work alongside the president of the commission and the high representative for foreign policy). More EU decisions would be made by qualified majority voting. Starting in 2014, double-majority voting would replace the voting system adopted in Nice, and the number of EU commissioners would be reduced. A Charter of Fundamental Rights, Freedoms, and Principles would be annexed to the treaty.

The parliament and the commission would, of course, with the systematic support of the Court of Justice, seek to ratchet up their powers beyond the letter of the Lisbon treaty. Although the general institutional balance of the EU would not fundamentally change, the treaty provides a framework and decisionmaking mechanisms that would enable qualified majorities to institute genuinely common policies in key areas such as immigration, justice, energy, and foreign policy. None of this is impossible under the Nice framework, but it would be more difficult.

Whatever treaties are in place, Europe can advance toward more common policies. However, even if Europeans are able to reach agreement on the budgetary and personnel issues, the process will gain momentum only if they are also able to agree on two major issues that continue to divide them: Europe's borders (and thus identity) and its strategy (and thus its role in the world).

What Boundaries for Europe?

Europe still doesn't know exactly what its physical boundaries are. What may be clear to Washington, Moscow, Beijing, Cairo, or Cape Town is not so clear to London, Berlin, Paris, Madrid, or even Brussels. History, geography, culture, language, religion— none of them can provide an authoritative map. So we all have our own definitions, and no one can impose a definition on others.

For decades, the division of Europe let Europeans get away with not having to decide its extent. It went without saying that the European Union was open to any democratic country in Europe. After the cold war ended, the need to embrace as quickly as possible those countries just liberated from communism substituted for a real strategy. But what now? Europe is so afraid of the identity issue that it is unable to define itself, whether according to its Greco-Roman roots, the Carolingian Empire, its Christian heritage, the Enlightenment and French Revolution, its proximity to the Near East, or its commitment to democracy and human rights. According to the 1993 "Copenhagen criteria" for EU membership, all that is required of a candidate is to be democratic, have a market economy, and accept established EU laws and regulations. But if those are the criteria, why not take in Senegal, Japan, India, and Brazil?

With all the back and forth over Turkish membership, the European Parliament and some EU governments came up with a fourth criterion: "absorption capacity," a sensible if inelegant notion originally proposed at the 1993 Copenhagen summit. The criterion was deliberately set aside by fourteen of the then fifteen EU members and by the European Commission, especially Commissioner for Enlargement Günther Verheugen, until 2006, when it was renamed "integration capacity." For just about everyone during that period, enlargement had become a moral (even more than political) imperative, to the point that even discussing it was seen to be politically incorrect.

But none of these criteria constitutes an identity, as Europeans know all too well. If the twenty-seven do not manage to get a handle on rampant enlargement—either because they cannot or do not want to—the European idea will be stretched to the breaking point. At that point the European Union will be something different: a vast Mediterranean-Eurasian zone of peace, stability, trade, and law topped off with a few common policies. This is far from nothing. Some would be very happy with such an outcome. But it would mean the end of "political" Europe, the abandonment of the goal of a common foreign policy beyond a few generalities about democracy and human rights. It would also mean the end of the notion of Europe as a global power on the same level as Russia or China and the end of a balanced partnership with the United States. If Europeans want to avoid this fate, they must have the courage to draw up a list of less than a dozen countries with an inclination to join the union when they—and the union itself—are ready. The list would certainly include the western Balkans and, if they so wish, Switzerland, Norway, and Iceland. The others would be subject to discussion even if they have already begun accession negotiations. After that, the enlargement would be complete.

As for Turkey, Europeans could have spared themselves many agonizing crises and unnecessary tensions if they had proposed to Turkey a "privileged partnership" before that term had become devalued. They could even have proposed a full alliance instead of trying to be nice by holding open the idea of Turkey's potential accession, which the Turks, quite logically, have seized upon to modernize their country. Since then, to avoid appearing anti-Muslim, selfish, and inward looking, the EU has not dared to refuse starting accession negotiations. Certain French and German politicians have even gone so far as to suggest that Turkey's entry, even though the country is officially secular, could serve as an antidote to the "clash of civilizations." (These are the same politicians, by the way, who deny the existence of such a clash.)

Preparing to harass Turkey for decades on every issue under the sun is not the proper way to treat that great country. The EU is trying to get Ankara to adopt the enormous set of legal norms it has adopted since 1957, plus some additional requirements it has invented along the way, even though the member states are clearly incapable of guaranteeing Turkey that, even after all this, they will ratify its accession. This is particularly true for France, especially since President Chirac—trying to reassure a hostile French electorate—had the French constitution changed to require a referendum for any new EU accession. France under Sarkozy modified this provision in July 2008, but a referendum is still required for enlargement unless a three-fifths majority in parliament votes to waive that requirement.

If Turkey is rejected or fails to qualify, what will be done? Will we go back ten years, amidst all the recrimination and bitterness, to the privileged partnership that we should have started with? Or will Turkey then say that EU accession no longer interests it and that it will simply pursue closer trade relations with Europe, reinforce its role in NATO, exercise its influence in Central Asia and the Middle East, and develop strategic relations with Russia, Israel, Iran, and China? For now, those "for" (Gordon Brown, the majority of member states, the commission, the parliament, and from the outside, the United States) as well as those "against" (Nicolas Sarkozy, Angela Merkel—albeit constrained by the CDU/SPD coalition agreement, and European public opinion) are hiding behind the negotiations under way. But that can last only so long. This is an example of the contradictions that result from muddled thinking about Europe.

Whatever they do about Turkey, Europeans have to admit that "Europe" is not a pure concept and that they must now define it politically and geographically. They have to set limits or accept the possibility that the union will come apart. Generally speaking—and barring a complete failure of the European project—Europe will probably end up fulfilling the theory of the three circles: a central core Europe, which already exists with the euro zone; a wider union consisting of thirty-five or more members; and associated countries—which former EU Commission President Romano Prodi has called the "ring of friendly countries"—to which the EU has offered a good-neighbor policy. The Mediterranean Union proposed by President Sarkozy in 2007 poses no additional enlargement problem. In fact, is has now been incorporated into the European Union's existing Mediterranean policies (the Barcelona process and Euromed). This merger should give new life to those policies, and the Mediterranean Union will take the form of a very flexible umbrella organization focusing on concrete projects.

In the end, the twenty-seven remain divided and uncertain about what the European Union's final geography should look like, a situation that creates unease and ambiguity about the union's future in the eyes of its citizens. For the British and others, there is still no need to define the ultimate limits of enlargement. As a primarily economic and commercial entity, they argue, the wider and more populous Europe is, the stronger it is. Thus Europe's interest is to take in not only the western Balkans but also Turkey and even other countries. The question of the EU's limits needn't come up, they argue, and even discussing it is futile and inconvenient. For example, Britain blocked discussion of enlargement by the Committee of Wise Persons on the future of Europe set up by President Sarkozy and presided over by former Spanish Prime Minister Felipe Gonzales. Those who favor new enlargements denounce their opponents' "cold feet" and accuse them of "turning inward." (How, by the way, can a grouping of 450 million people be inward looking?) Others also express the desire, shared by the United States, to align EU membership with NATO membership, even though the nature of the two organizations is very different. Supporters of indefinite enlargement thus want to break free from geography and history and to be able to define Europe by its openness to the global market economy (in which case, what would be the difference between the EU and the WTO?), its universal values (how would it be different from the UN?), or democracy (why not include Canada?).

On the other side of the debate are European countries, led by France, that insist that the EU's membership must at some point be stabilized. Otherwise its citizens will no longer identify with this fuzzy political entity in constant dilatation, a sort of subsidiary to the UN. It's not a matter of having "cold feet" but of political coherence. Does anyone accuse the Americans of having cold feet when they fail to propose that Canada and Mexico join the United States? Once its final borders are set, the EU will have good commercial relations and partnerships with its neighbors, but there will not be any new membership accessions. The position of Commissioner for Enlargement could be eliminated. This sort of clarification would have intrinsic political virtues. Ultimately, the right criteria for enlargement must be both geographical and political and they must be established soon. Otherwise the EU will remain politically weak.

What Strategy for Europe in the World?

Finally, Europeans are going to have to agree on the role that Europe should play in the world. The communiqués and declarations of the various EU-US, EU-China, and EU-Russia summits indicate that Europe is already a major power—in those documents, other great powers treat it as an equal, salute its global role, seek its support, and respect its decisions. In reality, however, that is all far from being the case.

First, when we talk about "Europe," what are we talking about? The council? The commission? The parliament? The twenty-seven governments? EU public opinion? The way each member state thinks about Europe? These are not all the same thing.

Second, being a great power requires more than having delegations in more than 120 countries, annually distributing 37.5 billion euros in foreign aid (of which 7.5 billion euros is managed by the commission), making declarations in favor of human rights, meeting regularly with American, Russian, Chinese, and other leaders, and defending common positions in the WTO. It also requires more than having—as dictated by the Lisbon treaty—a standing presidency, a president of the commission, and a high representative for the common foreign policy. And besides, outside

Europe no one is fooled: Berlin, London, Paris, Madrid, Rome, and Warsaw count as much as Brussels.

If ratified, the Lisbon treaty would alter this reality, but it would not make it disappear. To be sure, when the EU takes a position in the area of multilateral trade negotiations, Europe—with its 450 million consumers—is a great power, not just a statistical aggregation. Divergences among member states emerge in such matters whenever the negotiation gets difficult or the time comes for difficult compromises. Nonetheless, in the area of trade and competition law, Europe clearly is a major power, and companies around the world rightly fear its decisions. In other areas, however, Europe is not a major power, except when Europeans agree.

And I deliberately avoid saying "not *yet* a major power" because it is not at all clear to me that it ever will be one. The reason is that the issue of power is not only legal or institutional. It is a question of mentality more than the result of treaties. Since the Second World War, citizens of western Europe have believed in a post-tragic world, turning their backs on power except in the area of trade. They hate the idea of power, an attitude driven by their desire to overcome their past; and by their pacifism, idealism, hedonism, Atlanticism, and even historical exhaustion. They want to become a big version of Switzerland (even though the Swiss, in fact, have maintained a fighting spirit)—a rich, safe, protected area that takes humanitarian and philanthropic action through its NGOs. With the exception of France and Britain, they have relied on the United States to ensure their security, as consecrated in

NATO. That's the real reason so many other Europeans are distrustful about the French vision of European defense and of Europe as a major power. Why risk duplicating what NATO does? Why risk antagonizing the Americans? Why help the French recover their lost global role? This skepticism has led President Sarkozy to the idea of coming back fully into NATO to reassure other members of the alliance about European defense. But once France is back in the Atlantic fold, what motive will other Europeans have to support European defense?

Some European elites think they can escape this dilemma by focusing on Europe's so-called "soft power"—its commercial and legal influence and ability to set norms. But this is a misreading of Joseph Nye's concept of soft power, which acknowledges that the United States would not be where it is today if it did not also have "hard power." As Nye now explains, "smart power" is the art of combining both effectively. In other words, you need missiles and fast food, dollars and CNN.

After centuries at the top, much of the European public still assumes that Europe will maintain that position in the future. And since the adoption of the Maastricht treaty many European elites have assumed that Europe's role as a global power would automatically emerge from the 1997 creation of the Common Foreign and Security Policy (CFSP), from its legal dispositions, from the CFSP high representative (Javier Solana), and from certain common actions in places like Macedonia or the Democratic Republic of Congo. This is called the "step by step" approach. All of this would make sense if the world were made up of Europeans or small countries keen to get into the EU and thus willing to submit to its conditions for accession. But that's not the case. There are more than four and a half billion non-Westerners in the world, and the emerging multipolar world will not necessarily be stable, cooperative, and friendly. Moreover, Solana's remarkable efforts notwithstanding—and even without revisiting the enlargement issue—Europeans are deeply divided on foreign policy. We are a long way from the day when all Europeans have the same conception of relations with the United States, when Balts and Poles see Russia in the same way that western Europeans do, when northern Europeans put as high a priority on the Mediterranean as southern Europeans do, when the twenty-seven can agree on specific steps in the Middle East, or when Europeans agree on a coherent China policy.

And there is no simple institutional or procedural fix that can overcome these divisions. Europeans have no trouble whatever agreeing on general principles concerning democracy, peace, and human rights, but they do struggle to agree on concrete foreign policies. However, if Europe does not start acting like a realistic power, its weakness will render it dependent on the true world powers of tomorrow, whether states or other entities. Ultimately, it will not even be able to maintain its lifestyle. The European public's opposition to the Iraq war in 2003 was inspired by pacifism, not the quest for power.

So what should Europeans do? First, reject the notion that the question of Europe's role in the world has already been answered bureaucratically or procedurally, by declarations, treaties, or the December 2003 European Security Strategy. Instead they should have a real debate. European opinion across the board should be surveyed in a general referendum on the following question: "Do you want Europe to become a global power, given what that would mean in the areas of diplomacy and military affairs?" Such a referendum would set off huge and very useful discussions. It would be necessary to take the time to explain to Europeans what sort of power this Europe would be, how it would defend its legitimate interests and its ideas—all while working with multilateral and European institutions—to manage world affairs a bit better. The question of how Europe should relate to the United States and other major powers, as well as the question of how to manage globalization, would also have to be debated.

For decades, European federalists were certain that a globally powerful Europe would result from the end of the nation-state. But this never made any sense. Europe will not become a major power through the integration of weak and self-doubting nations but on the contrary through the convergence from above of the foreign polices of major European states—essentially a strategic agreement among Germany, Britain, and France. For a long time in France, the ideal outcome would have been for Europe to adopt the approach toward the United States it had taken since 1966–67: that of a friend and ally but an independent one. President Sarkozy is different—he thinks in terms of a "Western family."

Let us imagine that Europe comes to consider itself something other than a commercial, democratic, or philanthropic entity and that it develops a policy that is more than merely declarative, compassionate, or charitable. In other words let us imagine that Europe adopts a true foreign policy. What would the consequences be? The United States would no longer be able to single-handedly define the Western world's position or to impose all its decisions on its allies. For example, after September 11, the retaliation in Afghanistan would have been undertaken as it was, but the war in Iraq would not have been. The Israeli-Palestinian peace process would have really been advanced, despite all the pretexts found for not doing so and despite the huge and easily foreseeable obstacles created by Israeli expansion of settlements in the occupied territories even though a majority of Israelis accept the idea of a Palestinian state. If Europe had a real foreign policy, Europe and the United States would together, without giving up any of their demands, be talking to Iran as well as to all the protagonists in the conflicts in the Middle East and elsewhere. You only weaken yourself when you refuse to speak to adversaries that you cannot neutralize, as Nixon and Kissinger realized in the case of Mao's China, notwithstanding the differences between that case and those we face today.

The world would obviously have much to gain from a Europe that had become a pole in the multipolar world and if Europeans could agree on policies toward their neighbors; on a clear approach to Russia, the Arab world, China, Asia, Africa, and Latin America; on a smarter approach to terrorism; on how to promote democracy; on a post-Kyoto regime; on the Doha round; on UN reform; on the management of globalization; and on so many other issues. Everyone would benefit if Europe could form a true Euro-American partnership with the United States and prevent its American partner from drifting off into Western paranoia. All this can only come about if Europeans emerge from their dreams and the comfortable lack of responsibility and accept the demographic, environmental, and strategic challenges they face.

But even if the Lisbon treaty is eventually ratified, Europe's foreign policy disunity will not magically disappear. The broad consensus needed for Europe to emerge as a major power does not exist—it will have to be built. At the right moment, after all the necessary public debates and controversies, the question of Europe's role in the world would be addressed head on through a popular vote that would legitimize Europe's new global ambition. The Lisbon treaty was supposed to create a more favorable framework and context. But unless Europe can clarify its identity, its boundaries, and its strategy, it will continue to fail to reach its goals. It would also help enormously if the next U.S. administration supported the development of a stronger Europe.

The changing global balance of power could put Westerners—Americans and Europeans alike—on the defensive. Perhaps Americans think they still have all the means necessary to preserve their global leadership alone. But a European cannot help but think that a true and balanced alliance between Europe and the United States would be even better placed to intelligently defend their interests and values vis-à-vis "the Rest."

CHAPTER FOUR

France in a Globalized World

What about France? Instead of leading the process of European transformation that the world so badly needs, France has been going through a period of deeper and more insidious doubt than usual. Its loss of confidence has, in turn, contributed to Europe's own introversion. The essential question is whether this is just a passing phase or something more enduring.

A Loss of Confidence

I am not comparing the current malaise to France's colossal loss of self-confidence following the disaster of 1940. I believe this new uncertainty results from the evolving state of the world. France has been struggling to adapt to this evolution. In theory, there is no reason why France should be so troubled by globalization. Throughout its modern history, France has sought to be a model for the world. It has been ambitious and even adventurous. As a long-standing democracy, it should be glad to see the benefits of democracy and freedom spread more broadly in the world. As an advanced Western economy, it should, in principle, benefit from taking part in the unprecedented integration of other Western economies. As a country that has long taken a close interest in the "third world," it should be happy to see the development and emergence of nations that were dependent on others for so long. And yet, France feels ill at ease because it is unsure of—or dissatisfied with—its role in this new world.

The process of globalization that has been remaking the world for the past thirty years is not the same one that took place during France's first and second colonial empires. This time it is not being carried out by French soldiers, sailors, explorers, missionaries, teachers, or secularists. Nor is it being spread by great French intellectuals, lawyers, writers, and artists and certainly not by NGOs. In short, today's globalization does not allow France to project its ideas, values, language, and universal principles onto the rest of the world. Instead it is the rest of the world that is projecting itself onto France, and what's worse, the rest of the world doesn't find France very well adapted. France has lately been more the "globalized" than the "globalizer."

The globalization of the past few decades, in fact, has mostly been driven by the United States—its leaders, big companies, banks, investors, pension funds, and markets. It has been facilitated by incredible technological progress in the areas of information and the media, which can turn people all around the world into potential consumers for American goods, services, and symbols. For the past thirty years, this globalization with an American accent has also been based on a free-market ideology that has systematically reduced—and was even designed to delegitimize—the role of the state. It has portrayed any form of social protection as an unbearable handicap even as some salaries in the financial world have escalated to obscene levels. It has been conducted by a country with which France has at times had difficult relations because France has not always agreed to follow it blindly—and rightly so when you consider cases like Vietnam, the Middle East, and Iraq. Moreover, the United States has since 1945 occupied the place in the world that used to be France's—that of an example to the world. Faced with what they see as a sort of casting error, some French elites are jealous, even bitter. The fact that many Americans also have problems with globalization—and that majorities in *all* Western countries have a negative opinion of it— has done little to improve France's mood.

Yet even if we consider only the objective facts, this French loss of confidence is unjustified. Consider all that France still has going for it today: its role in international institutions and international politics; the expectations from all around the world of its foreign policy; its military capacities and credibility; its nuclear power, which not only provides an ultimate defense guarantee but which is proving to be a valuable means to limit global warming; its newly dynamic demographics; its industrial successes, including Ariane and Airbus; the extraordinary success of its global companies; the thousands of energetic French people living abroad;

the attractions of its countryside, its food, its wine, its fashion, its luxury industries, its quality of life and—regardless of what people say—its culture, language, intellectuals, architects, researchers, and writers. No matter. The French are still grumpy. If France is no longer at the center of the world—if it is now only an "average" power—what's the point? This assumption about France's status is in any case erroneous: if you consider the 192 members of the United Nations, France is not in the middle of the pack but rather is a globally influential power in a league with about ten others. Still, many in France wonder why it should heed all the calls for it to adapt to globalization.

The sentiment is all the stronger as many French no longer pin their hopes on Europe. For some, building up Europe as a global power would be a way of enhancing France's own power, and for many others, the concept of "social Europe" would guarantee French social protections and spread them to the rest of the continent. But no one foresaw that European integration would turn into a Trojan Horse for free-market globalization. They didn't imagine that France would constantly have to negotiate with its partners and that with majority voting—in principle desirable—France would always risk finding itself in a minority unless it made constant use of its diplomatic know-how and tactical skills. Those skills are considerable, but the situation is hardly gratifying.

The disappointment has in recent years turned into a form of self-denigration or even self-hatred. We've seen this in the area of the French economic and social system—I won't call it a "model"—and in its history.

It should be obvious that France needs to reform its economic and social system while preserving its essential features. A big EU state cannot fail to take account of the new laws of the global, competitive market economy nor can it follow economic, fiscal, and social policies too far out of step with those of its European partners. It is undeniable that France has lost ground to comparable countries in the areas of competitiveness and global economic performance. It is also clear that France's growing public deficits are becoming unsustainable and that they will weigh heavily on future generations. The fiscal strains have been pointed out not only by all the economists on the Right but increasingly also by those on the Left. And it is difficult to keep up with all the recent reports (by the OECD, Michel Camdessus, Michel Pébereau, Maurice Lévy, Patrick Artus, Jean Pisani-Ferry, Elie Cohen, and Nicolas Baverez, among others) that have concluded the same thing while also underscoring how France could benefit from a more open and assertive adaptation to globalization.

French advocates of the free market talk only of getting rid of archaic regulations and adapting to globalization. They are harshly critical of politicians on both the Left and the Right for failing to convince the French of the need for such reforms—as if this were an easy task. Some of these pundits go beyond the case for reform and take the self-examination to the point of rage, rejecting everything that is French. For them, everything is rotten: the French language, the legal system, the state, company management, political and cultural life, French traditions, and even the Republic itself. Those who hold this point of view voted for Nicolas Sarkozy in the 2007 election, even though his own view is more complex than that.

At the other end of the spectrum, some analysts claim to see nothing less than the pauperization of the middle class. They decry the growing gap between the poorest members of society and those who benefit the most from globalization. They see globalization as a zero-sum game. They condemn the degradation of the social fabric in which the situation of immigrant children and others who have not been integrated is one of the most glaring symptoms. Despite the social safety net, progressive tax policies, public schools and services, and social welfare programs, parts of the French population are not sheltered from the battering ram of globalization. Even the middle class does not feel secure. The French people I'm talking about here—who by the way do not vote only for the Left, far from it—see globalization mostly as a threat. Even though they benefit from globalization as consumers, they expect political leaders to protect them from it. If their leaders do not protect them, they reject them as incapable failures who don't "get it," and they vote against them in each successive election. Strengthened by this sense of insecurity, the French Far Left—which has no real equivalent elsewhere in Europe and which carries considerable electoral weight (some 10 percent of the vote)—invokes the "French system" as a shield against any efforts to adapt.

A harsher version of this self-criticism arises regarding French history. It is necessary for any people to understand all aspects of their country's history without any taboos. It is unhealthy to try to sweep the ugliest chapters under the rug, and it is perfectly normal to debate those issues. But that's not what has been happening lately in France. Discussions of the past have started to become rather masochistic. People are constantly "rediscovering" tragic episodes of French history as if they had somehow been hidden, which has generally not been the case. These episodes include slavery, colonialism, the mutinies of 1914–18, the Vichy regime, and the Algerian War. In each case, the goal does not seem to be to understand better, to learn lessons, or to teach new generations. Rather it is to level accusations as part of some atonement process, to obtain apologies or reparations, or to create new legal obligations. This process poses a number of ethical, political, and legal problems. What is the purpose of asking for an apology for acts undertaken by others in the past? To what degree is one responsible for crimes committed by one's ancestors? Is there such a thing, contrary to legal principles, as collective responsibility, and can this be transmitted over time?

The legal basis for such actions is highly questionable, especially since they're often put to political purpose with an obvious electoral or other self-interested agenda. At the other extreme, the same thing is true: the efforts to glorify France's past have similarly—and equally wrongly, for example on the subject of colonialism—taken the form of legislation. And yet laws designed to memorialize this or that episode have been passed at the behest of certain groups, over the objections of historians who fear the establishment of an official history that would outlaw research and punish heresy, much as an organized religion would do for violations of its dogma. These historians are demanding "historical freedom." We have gotten so far off track that the French National Assembly, though not the Senate, now claims to be able to pronounce the truth about the history of others—for example, in a bill supported by 106 members of parliament on October 12, 2006, making it a crime to deny the Armenian genocide. The French National Assembly is taking a position on the history of the Ottoman Empire? It's as if the Turkish parliament started passing laws about French massacres during the Algerian War. So when shall we vote on the extermination of American Indians? Whose parliament will go first?

There's nothing funny about this instrumentalization of history, but it's worth remembering that Darwin's contemporaries rejected the notion that humans had descended from apes. Today many Europeans—while hardly creationists—want to pretend that they did not descend from their ancestors and instead imagine an ideal history. If that's not possible they want to atone and repent in the name of those who came before them. All this suggests a country that is uncomfortable in its own skin, obsessed with getting revenge on itself, and destined to dwell on its past. But history is what it is. You've got to understand it, take responsibility for it, and overcome it. You must avoid self-flagellation as much as historical blindness or an air of superiority. The best antidote to the politicization of memory is good history. We must hide nothing, teach everything, communicate everything, and draw constantly updated lessons for the future.

The crisis in representative democracy, which is clearer in France than elsewhere, does not result from self-hatred alone, but the two tendencies are linked. The crisis results from some of the main characteristics of modern democracy: high levels of education, the spread of "infotainment," the proliferation of opinion polls, the need always to promise new economic policies, the acceleration of life in general, and a taste for "direct democracy." Because of all that, people are no longer willing to elect someone for a given number of years, trust them for that period, and then, depending on his or her accomplishments, support reelection or not. They are no longer willing to wait until the end of the term but instead want to weigh in on a real-time basis, give their opinion, and be consulted on all decisions in the name of direct democracy. And—except for certain activist voting blocs—they want to do this without even taking part consistently in the political process. Participatory democracy can just as easily discredit representative democracy as reinvigorate it.

For the twenty-five years prior to 2007 the French consistently voted for whatever party was in opposition, somewhat like an insomniac who keeps turning over in his bed. Now this French electoral discontentedness is being transformed into a general dissatisfaction with the entire French political system and its institutions. Thus have political leaders become scapegoats for everything—they take the blame so that others don't have to.

Among the most astonishing characteristics of this dissatisfied France is its constant underestimation of its own capacity for adaptation and innovation. Over a period of a few decades—the so-called *Trente Glorieuses* (Thirty Glorious Years)—this country that had been enduringly rural, protectionist, and traditional was opened up, Europeanized, and transformed into a creative economy of sophisticated industries and services. It is entrepreneurial, basically pro–free trade, and the home to many companies that dominate in world markets. The lifestyle has changed radically, even while remaining very French. In 2007 it was entirely possible that a woman would become president of the Republic. A large number of young French people go abroad to seek success. And this France is supposed to be threatened by globalization?

We have had many unproductive debates in France "for" or "against" globalization. Yet as opinion polls demonstrate, France is no more reluctant to embrace globalization than other Western countries. Besides, no Western country is either fully for or fully against globalization, and none wholly adapts to it or wholly shields itself from it. Everyone is affected by globalization whether they like it or not. Faced with the latest wave of globalization, all countries over the past thirty years have tried in varying degrees to take advantage of it, adapt to it, and innovate to take further advantage. But they've also sought to protect themselves at the global, EU, or if necessary national level when globalization threatened something essential (which is different for each country), just as they have sought to forge alliances to change the rules of the game (such as at the WTO or within various technical organizations). It's up to political leaders to find the right formula for their respective countries. Although it's not politically correct to say it, all Western countries have at one time or another put in place "protectionist" measures—which is not the same thing as embracing protectionism as a whole. They all, moreover, developed initially in part thanks to protectionist measures, and that includes Great Britain before it imposed its version of globalization in 1914.

France has all the potential in the world, but it has lost confidence in itself—in its ability to reform and recover. This makes no sense. Perhaps the 2007 presidential election campaign will have played a cathartic role.

A Foreign Policy Consensus?

French foreign policy has also been affected by this negativity. Although it allegedly benefited from a sort of consensus that went all the way from de Gaulle to Mitterrand, it has been increasingly contested of late, a process that prepared the ground for Sarkozy's call for change. In fact, the notion that French foreign policy had not changed since the beginnings of the Fifth Republic is a misconception. Its basic principles have indeed remained fairly constant: France has been faithful to its Western allies in times of serious crisis but otherwise autonomous and free in its actions. Beyond that, however, French foreign policy has evolved considerably.

Other than a small group of specialists (a much smaller group than in the United States), who really remembers the different phases? Who remembers French foreign policy under presidents Pompidou and Giscard d'Estaing? De Gaulle's foreign policy, on the other hand, has become a sort of myth that is presented as a bloc, when in fact it changed considerably over time. Initially—during World War II, for example—de Gaulle sought to get the United States and the United Kingdom to accept France as a third member of a Western directorate with a global mission. It was only after repeated rebuffs by Britain and the United States that he explored another path. The new path was symbolized by the 1961–62 Fouchet plans for political union (rejected at the time by stunned federalists but which would have served Europe well had they been fully implemented); by the 1963 Elysée treaty between France and Germany (which was then neutered by the Atlanticist preamble attached by the Bundestag); by the eventual withdrawal from NATO's integrated military commands; and by an independent French policy toward the conflicts in Vietnam, the Middle East, and Latin America. This approach—followed most aggressively by de Gaulle from 1966 to 1969—is supposed to represent the enduring nature of French foreign policy. In the first few years of this century, some felt it necessary to discredit that approach in an attempt to bring France into line with other Western states.

People are more familiar with François Mitterrand's foreign policy because it is more recent, it lasted fourteen years, and it was marked by big events (such as the end of the cold war), incontestable successes (European policy from 1984 to 1992), a number of controversial policies (toward German unification, toward the breakup of Yugoslavia, and toward Africa in general), and a huge polemic (over Rwanda). But even in those cases, has there been an honest and methodical evaluation of the results obtained and of the options available? Has France drawn the right lessons for the future? This form of rigorous debate is sadly less common in France than in the United States.

One could ask the same kinds of questions about foreign policy under the government of Jacques Chirac, which lasted for twelve years (of which five took place during "cohabitation" governments). In the public debate, the Chirac era comes down to the (justified) opposition to the Iraq war; the failure of the referendum on the EU constitution in May 2005; a controversial, "realist" policy toward Russia and China; and all too cozy relationships with certain Arab and African leaders. That view is too simple. The history of Chirac's foreign policy remains to be written.

Beyond the periodic criticism coming from the United States and a few other countries, French policy is denigrated in a number of quarters within France itself, including in the media. Despite the fact that French foreign policy is welcomed by three-fourths of the world, the argument seems to be that French diplomacy from de Gaulle to Mitterrand to Chirac has not changed and that it has now run out of steam. Such criticism is all the more dominant in the debate because the defenders of the classical conception of

French foreign policy—the defense of vital interests, freedom of action, and French influence—hardly speak up. These defenders include pretty much the entirety of French foreign policy specialists, but they play much less a role in the public debate than, for example, their American counterparts, as if there were something shameful or politically incorrect about their views or as if the media were not interested. By contrast, other activists have been working to change completely the main priorities and fundamental pillars of French foreign policy.

For Eurofederalists, who made up the hard core of the group of proponents of the EU constitution, the almost exclusive goal of French foreign policy should be European political integration with the ultimate goal of creating not just a common but a single European foreign policy. For this school of thought, any opposition to that goal can stem only from an archaic view of sovereignty that stands in the way of progress. Adherents to this school have been on the defensive since 2005, the year of the failed referendum, but they remain determined. Following the Irish rejection of the Lisbon treaty, they are going to have to make do with current institutional arrangements, at least for some time.

Then there's a "human rights first" school for which the promotion of democracy and human rights must be the top priority of French foreign policy and of Western diplomacy in general. This school is close to the American neoconservatives in terms of objectives but less so in terms of means. Some human rights defenders argue that we must press for human rights to be respected even without waiting for democracy to be well and widely established. That sounds great, but how to do it? They also judge French and other Western foreign policies toward Russia, China, the Arab world, and Africa according to this sole criterion. In France, this school is dominant in the media, on the Left (though not exclusively), and of course among NGOs. It refuses to accept the reality that foreign policies based on indignation and denunciation have mostly failed in the past. And it rejects objections to the dubious legitimacy of Western interference and interventionism, let alone neocolonialism. This school is somewhat bothered—though not too much—by the failures of American "transformational diplomacy" in the greater Middle East and elsewhere, an idea it could not help itself from sympathizing with initially.

One should also mention the "fundamentalist multilateralists," who, like Eurofederalists (though the two groups are not identical) believe that "France can no longer do anything by itself" and that its entire policy must be made in the context of the UN and other multilateral organizations. Ultimately, for this school, it's better not to act at all than to act alone. Its adherents also think that French foreign policy is too nationalistic, too traditional, and overly concerned with sovereignty. In this sense it's very different from the thinking in America in that even Democrats there are convinced that the United States, and therefore states in general, have a role in the world.

Even if inspired by a dubious desire to bring France's foreign policy into line with that of others, these critiques raise some

worthwhile questions. For example, it is high time to determine—
in a clear and durable way—the degree of integration among, and
the various roles of, EU member states. On the other hand, the
controversy over human rights is a red herring. Any Western foreign policy must of course have a human rights dimension, but
that doesn't really tell us—except in a posturing and rhetorical
way—how to act usefully and intelligently in this area. We have
seen this dilemma appear regarding Chechnya, Darfur, China,
and Burma. In the same vein, no foreign policy can be reduced to
this single dimension any more than it can be reduced to commercial considerations, culture, or the fight against terrorism. Unlike
NGOs, states cannot specialize. The nature of foreign policy is to
represent a sort of synthesis of priorities and choices. The defense
of human rights cannot alone constitute a foreign policy.

Finally, Chirac's foreign policy was the subject of virulent
attacks from the "Atlanticist" end of the spectrum, particularly
regarding the war in Iraq. It's not Atlanticist to want to engage in
normal cooperation with the United States—all French leaders
have been disposed to do so. It is Atlanticist, however, to reject—
under the pretext of wanting to combat allegedly deep-seated anti-
Americanism—any and all criticism of the United States, even if
it's well-founded and shared by a significant part of U.S. public
opinion itself. It's this school of thought that in recent years has,
under the cover of the "war on terror," channeled American neoconservative ideas regarding the Arab world despite their obvious
failures there. Some French neocons—on both Right and Left—

have not given up despite the American fiasco in Iraq and in the Middle East, the Republican defeat in the November 2006 elections, the difficulties of the Bush administration, and America's unpopularity around the world. This is the school of thought that stigmatized the very idea of France's "Arab policy," let alone the way it was pursued by Jacques Chirac. Is it possible that its proponents preferred Bush's Arab policy? This school also supports the American project of turning NATO into a global alliance. It is influential among current French elites and present in the Sarkozy government though not so widely supported by the French public as a whole.

At the same time, French foreign policy is now affected by a new set of constraints: puritanism and prudishness when it comes to protocol and diplomatic activity, as imposed by new censors in the media and elsewhere. Diplomatic measures are judged not by their utility in reaching a particular strategic or political objective but entirely according to how carefully they follow strict rules. You can meet with this person but not that one. You can deal with one organization but not another. You can go to one place but not others. You can shake one person's hand but not another's. You have to walk out of the room if someone says one thing but not something else. Diplomats have always employed these strategies, but with subtle distinctions so as to advance particular goals or get out of difficult situations. Under the watchful eye of those who shape public opinion, there are now so many things that are "not done" that the question is no longer "Is this useful?" but rather "Is it scandalous?" If it's seen to be scandalous, the indignity machine kicks into gear and creates a big fuss. Proper diplomacy cannot be conducted under these circumstances.

Manichaeanism and Western hubris have thus combined to create a bizarre logic: foreign policy has become useless because it is now used only for mutual congratulations among friends and allies, and one must not deal with pariahs or rogues. So instead we ignore them, sanction them, boycott them, or sometimes even bomb them! Yet it's just this sort of approach that is failing in the Middle East, even though diplomacy was invented so that you could talk to your adversaries as an alternative to war. Thus the Americans spoke to the Soviets starting in 1924, to the North Vietnamese starting in 1968, to Communist China starting in 1972, and most recently to North Korea; and France spoke to the National Liberation Front in Algeria, and Yitzhak Rabin worked with Yasser Arafat. What has become of the time when François Mitterrand could declare that "you make peace with those you are fighting" before the Israeli Knesset? President Bush, after four years of mistakes, went through the motions of asking the realists James Baker and Lee Hamilton for their advice, and they responded with courageous suggestions: focus U.S. troops on training instead of combat, and work toward a cautious withdrawal in 2008; reengage with Syria and Iran; get more actively involved in the search for peace between Israelis and Palestinians on the basis of two states; end the democratization mission; concentrate on defending American interests. Across the board, those recommendations were the complete opposite of everything the Bush administration had done up to that point. And for that reason, Bush could only ignore them.

At the same time, a traditional question about French foreign policy—what is a "leftist" foreign policy?—has lost its meaning. First, the language of diplomacy has itself become "leftist": everybody now talks about security, peace, conflict prevention, international cooperation, and development. Furthermore, it is clear that on many issues—Europe, the Middle East, Iran, relations with the United States, and Africa—divisions exist within the Left and within the Right in France. There are thus several alternative leftist foreign policies and several different rightist ones, as we have seen with the transition from Chirac to Sarkozy. The same could be said about the United States where Democratic and Republican foreign policies are concerned.

Serious global challenges lie ahead. It would make sense for France to stop pretending that it is not defending its interests, that it always speaks in the name of "Europe," "the world," the "community of nations," "peace," or "universal values." There are several reasons for this. First, it's not true. Like any other country, France has specific interests—those of 60 million French people. Second, no one outside France believes this line. It evokes only irritation or amusement. Third, it no longer flatters the French public but only disorients it. Defending its interests would not prevent it from simultaneously promoting its ideas about Europe or the UN, from exerting influence in ways the world appreciates, or from working together with its allies—on the contrary, that approach would be more honest, more convincing, and more effective.

Sarkozy's Foreign Policy

In May 2007, France elected Nicolas Sarkozy as president, with 53 percent of the vote, on a platform of making a "clean break" with the past. His election was the result of a successful effort to reunite the French Right, which had been divided since 1976 by constant infighting among its leaders. Sarkozy succeeded in taking advantage of a vague but intense desire for "change" at the end of the Chirac era. He siphoned off votes from the extreme Right by making a link between "immigration" and "national identity" that shocked the Left and by demonstrating extraordinary energy during the campaign. His adversary, Ségolène Royal, was unpersuasive and received only 47 percent of the vote.

Less than a year after his election, Sarkozy's popularity had fallen more than 35 percent, the biggest drop in confidence for a newly elected French president in such a short time. The decline can be explained, however, more as the rejection of the president's personal style than as a rejection of his policies—as evidenced by the relative popularity of Prime Minister François Fillon. Sarkozy has had some success with reforms, notably in the area of the "special regimes"—the generous early retirement plans for certain workers that President Chirac and Prime Minister Alain Juppé had tried and failed to modify in 1995. Sarkozy has also made some progress in modifying the status of commercial ports and extending the duration of retirement dues to forty-one years. The special tax on large estates and the thirty-five-hour work week have both been modified but not abolished. Other measures, concerning national administration, economic modernization, the education system, and national institutions are also under way.

As his popularity fell during 2008, Sarkozy made a virtue out of necessity and shrugged off his unpopularity. He insisted that he was elected to reform France and that he would continue to do so. The results would come in due course. Part of his electoral base regrets that some of his "rightist" reforms—lowering taxes on the wealthiest, extending the work week, and making the labor market more flexible—have not moved further and faster. And some leaders on the Left secretly hope that Sarkozy's necessary efforts to cut the budget deficit will make him unpopular before the next presidential election in 2012 (as happened to Gerhard Schroeder in Germany in 2005, when he lost to Angela Merkel). Sarkozy will himself boast of having reformed France after a long period of stagnation.

On economic policy, Sarkozy comes across as a pragmatist, mostly free-market oriented but also statist when necessary. He is also a pragmatist on Europe, like most other current European leaders. He demonstrated that by agreeing to avoid another referendum on the failed EU constitutional treaty, thus making possible its necessary renegotiation.

Sarkozy established several priorities for the French presidency of the EU (July–December 2008), including immigration, energy policy, global warming, and European defense. But whatever the plans for an EU presidency, events tend to intervene. Thus the global food crisis has boosted France's arguments for common agricultural policies, not only in Europe but perhaps in Africa and other regions as well. And the Irish rejection of the Lisbon treaty means that France will have to help find a pragmatic way forward on European integration. Such pragmatism will be more productive than was all the institution building of the previous decade.

More generally, Sarkozy has launched a far-reaching "Atlanticist" or "Western" reorientation of French foreign policy—that is, a foreign policy founded on a vision much closer to that of the United States or even the Bush administration. Naturally, the leadership in Washington is delighted. But what about the French? It is hard to know whether, preoccupied by their economic concerns, they will be indifferent, whether they'll rise up against this policy in a time of crisis, or whether they'll oppose it more generally. Or perhaps they will support it, out of hard-nosed realism.

Overall the French seem somewhat perplexed by foreign policy under Sarkozy and Foreign Minister Bernard Kouchner. Alongside some very welcome initiatives (the liberation of the Bulgarian nurses being held in Libya, improvement in relations with the new EU member states, sound management of the China-Tibet crisis, and energy policy), there has been some showboating (on

Lebanon and Darfur, for example). Contradictions have appeared between the humanitarian rhetoric and the realist practices on issues such as Russia, China, Libya, and Africa in general. The proposals for civil nuclear cooperation with a number of Arab countries are interesting but problematic. Some initiatives, such as the idea of a Mediterranean Union, have been excellent but marred by poor implementation. There are real questions about Franco-German relations, even if one cannot expect President Sarkozy and Chancellor Merkel to return to the type of special relationship that existed between Charles de Gaulle and Konrad Adenauer, Valéry Giscard d'Estaing and Helmut Schmidt, or François Mitterrand and Helmut Kohl. France's new foreign policy is still clearly in flux.

In the report I presented to President Sarkozy in September 2007 on "France and globalization," I recommended that France move beyond the fruitless debate about how to "confront" globalization and adopt a dynamic position "within" globalization. I suggested that France would rally behind a realist policy so long as we were clear about it. Such a policy would pursue openness to globalization, economic reform, and adaptation in combination with genuine solidarity for the victims of global competition, appropriate and temporary protection, and regulation at the European, multilateral, and global levels. It is wrong to see such policies in opposition to each other when in fact they are complementary. (The United States takes this approach much better than does Europe, which in its idealism runs the risk of coming across as the "idiot of the global village.") The balance among these different policy components could vary between the Right and the Left. President Sarkozy told me that this was the "theory behind his approach." Dozens of opposition leaders have said that the Left could base its own approach on this analysis.

It is entirely possible that Sarkozy will run for reelection in 2012 and win. But it would be wrong to believe that the French Left has disappeared. Its failings, contradictions, and absence of leadership after Mitterrand and Jospin are clear. Still, the Left's candidate did take 47 percent of the vote in May 2007. The Socialist Party (PS) won the 2008 local elections. Their leaders unanimously adopted a platform that makes the PS a party of the European Left comparable with others. It may lack a single leader, but it counts in its ranks a number of very talented people: Bertrand Delanoë, Ségolène Royal, Martine Aubry, Laurent Fabius, François Hollande, Dominique Strauss-Kahn, as well as Manuel Valls, Pierre Moscovici, Harlem Désir, Julien Dray, and other regional leaders and mayors. There is very little substantive disagreement among them, and they are proceeding in a determined way with the modernization of the party's program against a leftist minority (led by Henri Emanuelli and Benoît Hamon). One of these many talented PS leaders will become party secretary in 2008. Barring a major surprise (of the sort that we sometimes see in the United States), he or she, or one of the others, will be candidate for president in 2012—whether against Nicolas Sarkozy or someone else. This candidate will have to resolve the difficult issue of alliances for the second round: how to retain all the votes on the Left while winning over enough of the center to get beyond 50 percent? In any case, a more modern Left will be on the ballot in 2012 and will have every chance of winning.

In its own way, France is actively modernizing. But whether it's led by the Right or by the Left, it will always favor a better regulated and more humane form of globalization, one that does not create so much shocking inequality and which does more to solve the world's problems. In this sense France in 2009 may be more in sync with the United States than has been the case for the past thirty years.

CHAPTER FIVE

Conclusion
From Unrealpolitik to Smart Realpolitik

For some time after its victory in the cold war, the West thought that it alone was in charge of world affairs, the sole arbiter of good and evil. Now, more than twenty years later, it must understand that it no longer has a monopoly on history or power. Despite having promoted universal values and the rules of the free market, other world powers—which the West does not control and which have not forgotten the Western domination of the past 500 years—are on the rise. Aided by the very globalization desired by the West, they are emerging or reemerging with the intention of redesigning the world in their own way. Democracy and free-market economics will continue to spread but not necessarily under Western leadership or in a way that will guarantee Western supremacy. Neither competition nor politics nor history is over. On the contrary, the tectonic plates of geopolitics, geoeconomics, and geoecology have again begun to shift, and these enormous changes will not take place without significant disruption. We are entering an era of serious tensions. Westerners are going to lose, or perhaps have already lost, their monopoly. But they have not lost either their power or their influence, which could be considerable if put to use in the right way.

If the United States is unable to get beyond the hubris that led it astray over the past few years, it will create further disappointments and catastrophes, for itself and the West as a whole. With the 2008 presidential elections, the Americans must seriously analyze the causes of the failures of the Bush administration in the Middle East, including the deep conceptual reasons for this foreseeable fiasco. And the new administration will have to take a very different approach.

In 2006 the Baker-Hamilton commission gave the administration an opportunity—which it failed to seize—to adopt a more realist perspective on the world. So did former president Bill Clinton when, at the 2006 annual meeting of the Clinton Global Initiative, he declared that "in an interdependent world, it is impossible to get rid of all your enemies or occupy their territories. You therefore have to try to have more friends and fewer enemies. We need allies and partners. However powerful we may be, it is impossible for us to resolve all the world's problems alone." Let us hope that the Americans follow such wise advice, and soon. If they do, their global influence will be restored.

For their part, if the Europeans do not overcome their naïveté, they will be mere spectators of an unstable multipolar world being created without them. On the other hand, if they do face up to realities, they could by acting together become a major world power and true partner of the United States. A coherent and determined Europe would help compensate for the alarming vacuity of the notion of an "international community." Such a Europe would take account of the geopolitical balance of power and adapt its strategy accordingly. It could, for example, help promote global awareness of the environmental time bomb we are facing, which it has so far recognized more clearly than the United States. It could thus help transform the environmentally destructive economy of today into the ecological economy we need and make "sustainable development" a real policy as opposed to a slogan. Such a Europe could put the concept of solidarity among the world's six and one-half billion people on a solid footing since, whatever our divisions, we face the same threats. These ideas should be at the heart of the notion of "regulation" of untamed globalization and of the "global governance" so often praised in speeches. Europe is well placed to promote such thinking just as it can help rehabilitate the role of states and governments.

In a post-American, or "nonpolar" world, the strategic choice the West must make is whether to share power with emerging states. The long-term future of Western values and interests (which go together, after all) will depend in large part on the way in which it handles this issue. One option would be to oppose as strongly as we can the emerging states' challenge to Western supremacy—to ostracize anyone who defies the West, talking only to those we like, categorizing everyone as good or evil, and using sanctions, boycotts, military force, or democratization to impose the will of the "international community."

That option has been the approach of the Bush administration, which thought it could reshape the "greater Middle East." But it failed to do so and thus only accelerated the West's loss of legitimacy in the eyes of more than five billion non-Westerners, even if the United States continues to impress and attract because of its power and wealth. To reach its goals, the administration sought to maintain an atmosphere of permanent threat, vulnerability, and fear. It made the mistake of giving the terrorists the satisfaction of being named threat number one. It imposed a Manichaean view of the world by hammering home its simplistic vision. It sought to maintain total superiority in all aspects of political and military power. For a while, that approach worked all too well on American public opinion, while Europeans were always more skeptical. But that approach deprived the West of an extraordinary opportunity to spread its influence.

Alternative Western policies toward the rest of the world are possible. That is true not only with regard to the Muslim world but also with regard to the emerging powers, as many Americans themselves have begun to recognize.

The Muslim World

Where the Muslim world is concerned, Western policies must abandon the false, ideological, and self-interested position that denies the real importance of the Israeli-Palestinian problem. The tentative and illusory initiatives that came late in the Bush administration to deal with this issue (or at least to give the impression of doing so) change nothing. Not only has the West acted as if the clash of civilizations were inevitable, but it has made that clash worse even while denying its existence. It should not be surprising that such an incoherent approach has failed.

What must be changed? Where Israel is concerned, we must stop accepting the worldview of the Likud Party and its allies that there is no partner for peace. This thesis was invented by those who did not want to have to make territorial concessions. They did everything they could to ensure that the Palestinians would remain mired in chaos and division so that they could plausibly argue that the other side had no responsible interlocutor. And the strategy worked. It enabled the Israelis to avoid having to stop the expansion of settlements, to negotiate, and to compromise. And we can see the results: the ongoing worsening of the situation. The Palestinians and Arabs have for their part made numerous errors in judgment, tactics, and communication, but these have been secondary.

The West should support, encourage, and protect the large Israeli peace camp, which is composed of the more than 60 percent of Israelis who accept the principle of a Palestinian state but which has not, since Rabin's assassination, found a leader with the historical vision to achieve this difficult goal. As noted before, the paradox is that everyone knows what the solution is. As envisaged in the talks at Taba in 2000, it is two states, Israel and Palestine, living securely side by side. We must help promote the emergence of a new Rabin, or the equivalent of a Sharon before he was incapacitated—his political transformation would have taken him very far had his health not failed him at a critical time. The great tragedy is that if either Rabin or Sharon were still alive, the problem would probably have been solved by now.

Ruses such as the "Quartet," the peace process, big conferences, mediators, and special envoys only serve to maintain the illusion of progress. There is no point in talking continually about Israeli-Palestinian negotiations, which will always be futile unless the Israelis are determined to move forward. The Palestinians cannot withdraw the settlements on behalf of the Israelis! Nor can the Palestinians provide security guarantees. In the condition to which they have been reduced they cannot make any commitments in advance either for the Israelis or for themselves. To ask them to do so as a precondition for peace, as if they already had a functioning state (which will only be possible after two or three years, even with significant help), is cynical. An Israeli government that wants to resolve the problem must therefore be sufficiently strong to resist the violent attacks of those who want neither compromise nor peace nor withdrawals. It must proceed in the face of threats or perhaps even more attacks. It must keep in mind Rabin's brilliant and courageous statement that Israel must "fight the terrorists as if there were no peace process and pursue the peace process as if there were no terrorists." In short, Israel must not allow extremist minorities on either side to determine the course of events. And it must not stand in the way of a solution that would benefit Israelis, Palestinians, and the entire world.

To sum up, the interest of the entire West lies in sponsoring and supporting a process that can be launched only by a courageous Israeli prime minister. The process would continue with the conclusion of a negotiation (which would ultimately require the Palestinians to abandon the "right of return") and with the development of strict, credible, and durable international security guarantees for Israel as well as for the Palestinian state. It would require the courageous acceptance of a Palestinian state limited in size by a new Palestinian leader emerging from the process. The implementation of the final agreement will have to be backed with international supervision and engagement for a number of years.

What to do about Hamas, so often considered the obstacle to such a plan? First, it is worth noting that its current strength is the result of misguided Israeli and Western policies. By allowing the Palestinian problem to fester for so long (the territories have now been occupied for more than forty years), they have led the people to despair, weakened the nationalists, and bolstered the extremists and Islamists. Certain branches of the Israeli government played Hamas off against the Palestine Liberation Organization. The West also showed its incoherence in imposing free elections on the Palestinians and then refusing to recognize their results, even though those results were easily foreseeable given the corruption of the Fatah government and the unbearable living conditions.

Denying the reality of Hamas only handicaps Western policy further. The way to deal with Hamas now—to bring it along, divide it, and eventually get beyond it—is by developing a real process that astutely involves Hamas. How can it be done without undermining the Palestinian Authority, whose utility the West has now discovered? It can be done by improving, as the Palestinian Authority constantly demands, the unbearable lives of the Palestinians, which would include addressing the issue of security checkpoints.

Such a policy would require courage and perseverance because many will seek to oppose it. But it is not unrealistic. And certainly nothing is more dangerous than the current status quo, which—by generating images on the evening news every day that enrage the Muslim world—deepens the gap between the West and Islam and undermines the "war on terror."

The creation of a Palestinian state is not a generous gesture to be undertaken only if the Palestinians behave and fulfill impossible preconditions! It is a right for Palestinians and a strategic interest of Israel and the West.

A solution to this burning problem would not resolve everything, but the relationship between Islam and the West cannot really be improved without one. It would finally make possible plans for Middle East development of the sort periodically put forward by people such as Shimon Peres and King Abdullah of Jordan. The spiral of peace and modernization would extend to Syria—and therefore to Lebanon—and transform them. The image of the United States and the West would be quickly and profoundly enhanced in much of the world. Israel would be relieved of a problem that weakens it and weighs heavily on its foreign policy. It would gain considerable influence, including among Arab governments and Palestinians who want to improve their ties with the West but cannot so long as the unbearable status quo endures. Israel's external enemies (such as Iran, Hezbollah, and al Qaeda) would see the power of their rhetoric diminished in the Muslim world. Terrorist recruiters would be undermined. The clash of civilizations would suffer a real setback, which would make possible other big successes.

Although such a strategic turnaround depends on more than just the United States (other countries and groups must promote and support it), it is to the United States that Israel—and perhaps also the Palestinian state—will turn for support and security guarantees. Many American officials know perfectly well that solving the Israeli-Palestinian problem is essential and that America's ability to play a crucial role in the process is in fact one of the strongest cards in the American deck. Seen from Europe, it is difficult to understand why the United States does not play it.

A different approach toward Iran is also necessary. One has frequently been proposed in recent years, and not only by James Baker and Lee Hamilton. It's not a question of naïvely going from a policy of pressure to one of fraternization but of abandoning posturing in favor of a policy that could break the stalemate. Given that the policy of ostracizing Iran in recent years has weakened and

exasperated it without forcing it to renounce its objectives, changing that policy could prove to be a useful innovation for a new
American president. The United States could propose uncondi-
tional talks with Iran on all the relevant issues—nuclear, security,
sanctions, Iraq, Afghanistan, and others.

Recent history has shown that insisting on preconditions for
talks tends to backfire against those who lock themselves into such
positions, except, of course, in case of total war. Diplomacy was
not invented for self-congratulation but to communicate, when
it's in your interest to do so, with determined adversaries whose
values you may reject but whom you cannot make disappear. Talks
are neither a gift nor a seal of approval but a lever. When its
intransigence has failed, the United States has always ended up
speaking to its adversaries (except during World War II, a real
war). Now, after all the silly triumphalism, the time seems right to
recalibrate U.S. diplomacy.

Why does the United States follow such self-paralyzing, backward policies when it comes to the Middle East? Apparently out of
a mix of fear and ideology. But why deprive yourself of the advantages of an active strategy? A U.S.-European initiative toward Iran
would put Iran's leaders on the defensive (whereas the strategy of
isolation has mostly helped President Ahmadinejad), and it would
provoke all sorts of divisions among them. They would have to
decide whether to talk, who should talk, and about what. Traditional Iranian nationalists would gain leverage, as would the West.
Of course any negotiations would have to be handled carefully,

with a mix of carrots and sticks. The objective in the nuclear arena would be to try to get Iran to accept a status like that of Japan. America's allies would support such an approach. In July 2008, the Bush administration took a few small steps in this direction, but a more far-reaching conceptual and strategic change is necessary.

Policy toward Afghanistan must also be significantly redesigned. It makes sense to keep the military pressure on the terrorists to prevent their reorganization. At the same time, none of our political, economic, or humanitarian objectives can be reached unless we change course. And that means accepting some Afghan realities. One of these is that that we'll have to deal with players other than the Afghan government: the British have now understood that we must get the Pashtuns—including some former Taliban—more involved and that we need a more sophisticated approach to Pakistan.

On Iraq, it would be a lie to pretend that anyone has a miracle solution. A precipitous American withdrawal would inflame the civil war and could possibly lead to the breakup of the country. The United States can leave only if it succeeds in doing what it didn't do before the war and what it has failed to do afterward: achieving a political agreement among the various Iraqi communities with institutional guarantees on oil and finances. And this can be done only with the involvement of neighboring countries, which means we must talk to them. Then and only then will Iraqis be able to get the assurances on oil and security they need and that the Americans need in order to withdraw.

In a general sense, the United States must learn the lessons of the failure to impose democracy by force from the outside in countries where democracy has no roots and where relations with the West remain colored by colonialism. The idea of remaking the Middle East by promoting democracy was beautiful. It even seduced many Democrats to the point that some of them still today dream of creating a League of Democracies independent of the UN. But against whom and to do what? I'm afraid the West is going to have to accept that it can no longer impose the regimes it wants any more than it can artificially create nations from the outside. Does this mean just resigning ourselves to autocracies and burying our democratic aspirations? No. But the promotion of democracy needs to be put on a longer-term footing. Instead of simplistic and often brutal policies that are based on force and ignore local realities, we need a smarter policy that takes advantage of the potential for democracy in every society, even the most stagnant and archaic ones. Such a policy could take the form of a partnership for political and economic modernization with those in the region who are ready to move in that direction. There will be more of them than many realize, especially if an Israeli-Palestinian agreement is reached. What I'm proposing here is a turn away from ideology and a return to politics. Countries like France, Britain, and other European states have experience and ideas that could be put to good use in such a move.

ভ৹ ভ৹ ভ৹

The West's strategic priority must be to stop gratuitously fostering the clash of civilizations, which only plays into the hands of the extremists. But even beyond that, the United States and Europe must rethink the entirety of their approach to emerging powers, big and small. Americans and Europeans alike have struggled to prioritize their goals when it comes to countries like China, Russia, India, and Brazil. These countries are variously seen as markets, partners, competitors, adversaries, threats, and targets of democratization—thus the perception of confusion and contradiction in Western policy. Meanwhile the emerging powers themselves are moving forward with their own, often very clear, strategies. And those strategies no longer require Western permission. Alliances and links among the emerging powers are also developing rapidly, without involvement from the West.

The West's interest is thus to agree on realistic, clear, and durable policies toward each particular emerging country. Such policies must recognize the power those countries already have, their legitimate right to development, and their potential, but they must also include the no less legitimate right of the West to defend its vital interests, values, and convictions—even while understanding that these cannot be imposed on others. Western strategy must accept new forums for dialogue and negotiation, the reform of international organizations, and proposals for new international rules. And this approach must be pursued on a consistent, long-term basis.

In 1945 the United States led in the creation of a world order that American leaders had been thinking about since the start of the war, drawing on the lessons of the League of Nations. The challenge today is even greater in that the outcome will not be negotiated by two or three victors but by a large number of countries—established powers, emerging or reemerging powers, regional groupings, and ordinary member states of the United Nations that are themselves influenced by the many so-called new actors in international relations. There will not be a single San Francisco conference nor a single Bretton Woods or Havana conference, nor a single special conference of the United Nations. Rather there will be multiple negotiations and skirmishes stretched out over time. There will be specialized meetings and general meetings, with ups and downs and breakthroughs and setbacks, all influenced by economic and environmental factors. Alliances will be formed and broken, and there will be an infinite number of disagreements among Western powers, just as there will be among the emerging powers. All this will play out at the UN, the IMF, the WTO, the G-8, and elsewhere, including in the area of economic competition, taking place in the shadow of potential environmental catastrophe.

The West must agree on a realistic and strategic vision of these coming changes to avoid disagreements between the United States and Europe that would weaken both. The United States has nothing to gain from divisions within Europe, which could lead to splits between Washington and some European states on how to deal with particular emerging powers. After eight distressing years, the arrival of a new American administration is a good time to rethink transatlantic relations. Europeans are fascinated by—and expect much of—Barack Obama, whose election would have an impact all around the world. At the same time, Europeans respect John McCain. Regardless of which one gains the White House, Americans and Europeans will have to forge a new strategic alliance based on smart realpolitik. Europeans must urgently prepare for such a transition, and Americans need to think about what they could bring to the table. The stakes are enormous.

Index

125